RONALD RA

JOSEPH ESCAPES

TO GLASTONBURY

Mysticism and Superconsciousness
Spiritual and Physical Healing
Parapsychology
Scrying with the
Skull of Doom
The Sercret of The Holy Grail
Achieving Independence
for Ukraine

BLACKTHORN PUBLISHING

Author Ronald Rayner with Wilson the Skeleton
wearing the Urim and Thummin

DISTRIBUTOR
Add Design
Britannia House
Bentwaters Business Park
Rendlesham
Suffolk IP12 2TW
United Kingdom
Telephone: (UK) 01394 460600
E-Mail: info@add-design.co.uk

ISBN 978-0-9557906-2-1

PUBLISHER
Blackthorn Publishing Ltd
Suite 404, Albany House
324-326, Regent Street,
London W1B 3HH
United Kingdom

Printers:
Colt Press Ltd, Unit 7C Perry Road, Witham, Essex CM8 3UD UK

Some of the photographs and drawings in this book are based on ideas as opposed to real events

ACKNOWLEDGEMENTS

The author owes a debt of gratitude to his wife Sylvia Rayner, Lady of Annesley Grange, Nottinghamshire, for all the research and translation that made this book possible.

Glastonbury Saints
by
Sylvia Rayner

Typist: Susan Thomas.

Photographs and Sculptures
by
Craig Rayner

Wilson the skeleton
Curse casting skull
Rough cast bronze cross
Arm bone from Glastonbury
Skull of Doom
Armageddon Skull
Crystal Skull
Carvings of Good and Evil (back cover)
Shaman Spirit Doll
Carving of Joseph of Arimathea

The writings of
Rev. R.W. Morgan
Rev. Lionel Smithett Lewis M.A.
Artist Eustace Nash
Drawings by Horace J. Knowels

Every effort has been made to trace publishers of extracts used from our ancient library. One or two dissappeared from records during the war years. To them we offer our thanks.

INTRODUCTION

I did not set out to write books and make documentaries with the purpose of attracting fame and fortune. My prime objective for my writing, and my films, is to make a difference. I achieve this by introducing into people's lives that which is clean, wholesome, good, and beautiful. I work with personal conviction, to trigger betterment in everyone who comes into contact with my work. My efforts are also planned to bring about beneficial change in the way in which some people may lead their lives.

I enjoy putting people in touch with extremes of emotional realities surrounding subjects that may have held an appeal at sometime in people's lives, or about which people may have been curious. I start out using instances of highs and lows of powerful convictions in history. I knit these together in a factual unbiased way that fetches eternal truths to the surface. Truths of pain or love that are so fundamentally important they cut through the mire of artificiality and pretence that saturate us in our daily lives. Truths that have the power to bring about changes in thought patterns, and values, in a way that can set people free. Those who are set free may then exude a power from within themselves that cannot be ignored by thinking minds around them.

I know from reader's letters that my overall strategy is successful in shining through for some. Literally switching on a light in a very dark tunnel, in which they felt trapped.

I am sometimes sad that I see people in the world waiting in droves for good news that will never arrive. They sit slowly being overtaken by a shadow, a shadow being cast by future events that will affect their lives for the worse. Sitting with eyes wide open but unable to see that the time to change their thinking to redefine what really are the true values or worth in their lives and in the world, is now.

Prime numbers will, over time, explain the secrets of the Universe, but they will never explain the Holy Spirit. Breakthroughs to ultimate truths outside the realms of science will come from writers like myself, who steer their way across the various disciplines, unconstrained by what is institutionally or politically correct, who will show, beyond doubt, that life on this planet came from Divine Plan, and not a spark of chance.

Many people have a deep longing to know or hear of that which is extraordinary; the eternal truths are out there, however, but are only seen by those who have the eyes to see.

Ronald Rayner, Vienna, 2009

THE
JESUS SCROLL

INDEX

Title	Page No.

ENGINEERING UKRAINES INDEPENDENCE FROM THE SOVIET UNION

In 1991 Ukraine declared its independence from the Soviet Union. The announcement was followed by the election of the country's first freely elected President and Parliamentary Deputies. This was the final act in changing the future history of the newly Independent Sovereign Country by pointing the destiny of its people and economy towards political freedom. Ushering in a free market economy.

The key to unlocking the door to the free world for Ukraine was the arrival in the Capital City Kyiv, of the man I have personally regarded as America's greatest and most successful President, together with his team.

The first step in the U.S. President's blueprint in bringing about a new future for Ukraine, was to secure all the nuclear warheads in storage and fitted to a multiplicity of intercontinental ballistic missiles sitting in silos on Ukrainian soil. The second part of the U.S. President's plan was to ensure that all Ukrainian missile silos were destroyed, in order to prevent their future use and their acting as a tool for threatening the West.

The U.S. President announced that in order to bring his plans to fruition, Ukraine must declare its independence from the Soviet Union and become a Sovereign State. The independence would be both political and economic and Ukraine would bring its military forces, together with their assets and hardware, under the control of the new Ukrainian Parliament. Ukraine's, KGB, university graduates to a man, had done their homework. They informed the U.S. President that the people in all the key positions throughout Ukraine were all in accord with the idea of a new way forward for Ukraine.

Those running the big industries in Ukraine, senior KGB, Army, Navy and Air force Chiefs, in addition to diplomatic staff, were all coming round to the same idea. That it was time for industry, commerce and the people of Ukraine to enjoy the fruits of democracy, and the only way that could happen was for Ukraine to gain complete independence from control by Moscow. The alternative was for Ukraine to remain the bread basket, iron foundry and coal mine of the Russians, when all the valuable resources and wealth in Ukraine would continue to be sucked into the Soviet Union without Ukraine receiving anything worthwhile in return.

The Deputy Head of the KGB informed everyone present that in his opinion Russia would respond to Ukraine's Declaration of Independence by declaring the Ukrainian currency as worthless and then cut off supplies of goods to Ukraine. The effect would be to close the doors on sales by the retail industry temporarily, whilst at the same time open up new opportunities in the internal economy for anyone who had the knowledge, experience and ability to take advantage of the situation.

The Ukrainian KGB officers spelt out to the meeting all the possible problems and difficulties ahead. The CIA were ahead of events. They had already briefed the U.S. President who had prepared solutions which were as follows.

The United States Government would purchase all the plutonium harvested from the dismantling of all Ukraine's atomic warheads. The U.S. dollars paid for the plutonium would enable Ukraine to issue its own currency tied to the U.S. dollar. In the meantime Ukraine should issue a temporary coupon which would be exchanged for a new currency, when America had received the Plutonium and paid over the U.S. dollars to Ukraine.

The Americans said they would ask Britain to provide instructors, based with NATO, to train Ukrainian Special Forces based around the Black Sea Ports, to prevent any retaliatory takeover by the majority Russian population living in those strategically important areas. Both Germany and France would be kept in the dark about the plans, for obvious reasons.

The announcement itself would need to be carefully timed. It was decided to make the Declaration of Independence from Ukraine's largest Aircraft Carrier during an important International Athletics event staged on the Aircraft Carrier and televised worldwide.

The Athletics event would be named

Extensive intelligence gathering revealed that with the Soviet Union disintegrating, and almost bankrupt, the Russian Generals did not have the stomach for and would not support an invasion of Ukraine. A country with which everyone had enjoyed good relationships for many years. Whose forces the Generals knew would put up a good fight. Many lives on both sides of such a battle would be lost and the likely outcome was a stalemate. One of us remained on the Aircraft Carrier to observe events. History was in the making.

Jubilation as Ukraine Becomes an Independent Sovereign Country

U kraine becomes an independent sovereign country. A new temporary currency, a coupon, was introduced and would suffice until America paid over U.S. dollars for the plutonium from the missile warheads. A new replacement currency, the Ukrainian Grivna would be rolled out.

A British Merchant Bank was given the task of setting up Air Ukraine on commercial lines to make daily return flights from Kyiv to London Gatwick Airport. A cargo plane was scheduled for weekly return flights to Gatwick Airport. Within weeks U.K. and Irish businessmen were travelling to Kyiv to explore business opportunities in that newly opened region. Obtaining a visa from the Ukrainian Embassy in London.

Sylvia and I took the wives and staff of Ukrainian Diplomats on shopping trips to the Lakeside and Bluewater shopping centres in Essex and Kent. They usually stood in stunned silence looking over such a great abundance of shops and goods. However they were put off shopping at the Bluewater Centre in Kent when they saw an obvious police presence, reminding them of the Soviet era.

The whole scheme for an independent Ukraine devised by the Ukrainian KGB and Military, CIA and MI6 was brilliant. For the Americans it was a coup. The closing down of a formidable array of intercontinental ballistic missiles fitted with atomic warheads, plus the destruction of the missile silos was bought at a small cost for pulling some of Moscow's main teeth for threatening the West.

We flew to Cyprus with a very senior intelligence officer in charge of the Missile silos. He was to be debriefed before starting a new life in America. He told us he was relieved at the handover. He said that he was not confident that, were the missiles to be launched, one would not fall back on to the silos and others might never leave Ukrainian Air Space. Another part of the deal was that Sylvia and I would meet his young son at Gatwick and take him to Bath University to study for a degree in English.

At that time hotels in Cyprus were flooded with Russians because it was the only place in the world where Russians could bank their money without too many questions being asked, and obtain an Entry Visa on arrival.

I was surprised to see Iraqis in our hotel bar. I asked the waiter to place my coffee and sandwiches on a window ledge beside their table. I went over to retrieve my coffee and food and saw that they were pawing over drawings of Shoulder to Air Missile Launchers.

The only problem that revealed itself as a result of Moscow cutting its ties with Ukraine was a shortage of clothing and consumer goods.

View of old Kyiv from the Czar's Garden 1843.
Watercolour by Solntsev, Fedor (1801-1892).

Ukraine Signs an Accord with China

Sylvia, myself and my youngest son Craig, who had just finished his SAS survival courses, flew to Hong Kong where we spent a year setting up supply chains to Ukrainian Black Sea Ports. A shipping time of four weeks for containers from Hong Kong.

After six months living in the Kowloon Shangri La Hotel and working seven days a week, I was approached in the hotel restaurant by a man who owned a famous fish restaurant in town. We were invited to a meal in his restaurant that evening. Apart from the man and his wife, the guests were three Chinese Intelligence Officers, who said that the Chinese Government were very pleased with the business from Ukraine and would like us to meet their bosses. Next morning we met in the Banking Hall at the Bank of China, went upstairs through clanking doors and grills to the triangular bit on top of that high building. First the officials, drinking copious amounts of Jasmine tea, said that they were aware we were known for our integrity and honesty, recommended at highest government levels.

The main purpose of the meeting was to examine ideas to secure further business from Ukraine. I recommended that they send a senior official to Kyiv to arrange the Signing of an Accord with the Government of Ukraine and address the newly elected Parliamentary Deputies. This was duly arranged.

The Senior Deputy said that there will come a time in the future when China would be lending aid monies and business loans to both Britain and American Governments. His other preoccupation was with the idea that Sylvia and I should travel round world airports to look for hotels that could be taken over for Chinese Tourism. China, he said, could flood the world with tourists if only 1% of the Chinese people were allowed to travel. He also enquired about the possibility of his son learning English and being educated at Bath University.

With the job done and my blood pressure raised from overwork and eating too much monosodium glutamate in Chinese food, we decided to fly back to the U.K. for a rest. However, before we left a telephone call informed me that there would be hundreds of millions of dollars in work when the new airport was officially given the go-ahead. I knew that in Britain this information would fall on deaf ears because it would not be 'easy money'.

THE MAFIA AND ITALIAN SHOES

After a few days rest we transferred to Italy to set up a supply chain for mens, womens and childrens shoes, plus some upmarket leather jackets.

Italy was a very different experience to Hong Kong. In Hong Kong nothing stopped or closed. It was possible to go to Temple Street Market in the early hours of the morning to buy Louis Vuitton bags, Chanel scarves, clothes made to fit while-u-wait. For a couple of dollars a bird would pick an envelope from a rack that contained details of the future or a Chinese would clean the wax from ones ears while seated on a chair at the kerbside.

ARRIVING IN VERONA ITALY

A black Mercedes and a Secret Service Agent were placed at our disposal to drive us the length and breadth of Italy to the largest footwear and clothing factories in the country to secure business that would help an economy in recession.

Our first purchase of shoes was from a factory outside Verona. I ordered in two forty foot tilt trailers from Poland. The running time from Verona in Italy to Kyiv in Ukraine was around five days. However, I had been given a tip-off never to acccpt the loading of shoes from an Italian factory without examining boxes as they were loaded.

Sylvia and I bought two loads of shoes on visiting our first factory. Price was important. Every one dollar saved was a big benefit in those times to retailers in Kyiv, when a dollar really mattered. I gave clear instructions to the Directors of the footwear factory not to load the tilt trailers until Sylvia and I arrived to inspect the loading.

We arrived at the factory at 8am the following morning to discover that contrary to my instructions both lorries had been fully loaded. We became suspicious, added to which we could not find anyone around in the factory although the doors were all unlocked. The Polish lorry drivers were sleeping soundly in the lorry cabs. In order to allay my suspicions I climbed onto the rear of the lorry and threw down a carton. The carton burst open and shoes spilled out onto the factory floor. Some shoes were so old the lace up eyelets had turned green, staining the leather. I threw down the next carton. Sylvia called up to me that the carton was full of gym shoes. The noise we were making wakened the drivers.

Factory staff also started to appear. A very very fat man called down from a rail outside his office, "give me the Bankers Draft and I will release your lorries so they may get underway". The Director clambered down metal steps to the factory floor. I took the Bankers Draft from my inside pocket and tore it slowly into small pieces in front of him. "These are not the shoes Sylvia and I had chosen very carefully for Ukraine. Furthermore, I gave you strict instructions not to load until our arrival". His reaction was immediate. He went ballistic. So much so that his whole body reverberated with shaking fat. A spectacle that sent the Polish lorry drivers into hysterics, almost collapsing onto the floor. This was unhelpful.

The Italian Shoe Factory Director screamed at us, "I am going to call the Mafia: They will force you to pay up". He then ordered the factory gate, driven by a very slow motor, closed. Trapping us, our Mercedes and two lorries into the factory compound. I responded calmly "This is Russian money and if you think you are going to force money from us, think again. I will call the KGB and a unit will be on its way here from Rome and, compared with the KGB, your Italian Mafia are pussy cats".

I beckoned our Mercedes driver and said to him "You are Secret Service, call the Police and have us released from here". To my astonishment he said "I cannot do that. This is not a police matter. It is a civil matter and I know these people". I looked across to Sylvia. We walked to the two bemused Polish drivers, who had unloaded the lorries. I showed them the 400 U.S. dollars I had in my pocket, about a year's wages in Poland. We handed them the money. And with an understanding nod, thumbs up, a Polish hand shake, the lorry took the gate off its mount. We jumped into the Mercedes and sped through the entrance. We were clear and freedom beckoned.

Fortunately, on the way to Verona, my Italian was sufficient to spot another shoe factory. We rushed into the reception, and a man who turned out to be the owner was standing at the desk stroking the receptionist's back. I explained our experience blow for blow at the factory about five miles back. You were in a mafia owned factory. He urged us not to worry because we could park our lorries at the rear of his factory, choose whatever footwear took our eye. His staff would load the lorries and the lorries could be on their way to Kyiv, Ukraine. "I know about your buying trip. We were informed by our local Chamber of Trade. I know we will be paid". With that he ordered us up to his office for a bite of lunch before setting about the task of choosing and pricing shoes.

Meanwhile our Polish lorry drivers were happily choosing shoes, 'T' shirts and other clothing for their families back home. Showering with the water from their tanks and enjoying the break.

THE QUEEN AND CBI

Sylvia and I decided to fly back to the U.K. for a few days. We had rented a house with a built on swimming pool with rooms over. Ample space where newly appointed diplomats could stay from a Country that was not yet fully recognised and had no real currency. Situated in a pretty Essex village with yacht clubs and only one road in and out where the coming and goings of limousines with darkened windows would not be noticed by the locals.

At Midnight on the day we had returned to our house in the U.K., I received a telephone call from our Embassy, relaying the information that the newly elected President of Ukraine had arrived in the U.K., that evening. The plan was to sign an Accord with the Conservative Prime Minister, enjoy dinner with Her Majesty the Queen and address the CBI.

The Ambassador's request was for me and Sylvia to meet some of the party at Austin Reed in Piccadilly, London next morning at 9.30am to ensure that the party was suitably dressed for the occasion. Unfortunately on that morning there was an explosion in the area to which we were travelling, which I suspect was meant for our party.

The Ambassador, a tall well dressed very intelligent man for whom I have the utmost respect, was fine. However, one of the group was smartly dressed in a hacking jacket, trilby and jeans. This would just not do for Buckingham Palace. I telephoned a man who was a Secretary to Her Majesty, and with whom I had worked when he was a newsreader with the BBC. The instructions were clear. Dark grey suit, white shirt, dark maroon tie, black Cambridge style shoes and the appearance would be fine.

Sylvia and I politely turned down an invitation to remain with the party because we did not want to see our photographs in the national press which could place our lives in danger.

After their last appointment addressing the CBI, the party returned to our house before heading for the Airport to return to Ukraine where there was much work to be done. Sylvia and I were asked to return to Italy to meet an aircraft carrying Ukraine's National Athletics Team. On board was a textiles expert who would travel with us through Italy to select clothes suitable for export to Ukraine. The new daily Meridiana flight from Gatwick to Verona made travelling easy for us. The flight from Gatwick to Verona was just over one hour duration, after which we were driven to our destinations throughout Italy down as far as Bari.

Shortly after arriving in Bari we were told there was a high ranking Italian Mafia group looking for us and that we should leave immediately. Our contact drove us straight to Bari Airport, where there was a plane on the tarmac waiting to depart for Rome. We boarded the plane and ignored a torrent of abuse from the Italian pilot for delaying the departure. At least we were safe, but making an unnecessary journey to Rome at the time of year when it was too hot for we English to enjoy the occasion.

As always in life, fate takes a hand. I recognised the wife of a Ukrainian Athlete. She lived in Kyiv, and to whom we had been introduced at an embassy in London. After the seat belts sign went off she jumped up and greeted us with yelps of joy and moved into the empty seat beside us. She was flying to Rome to meet her husband who had missed the flight. She showed us that her luggage she would be taking was contained as usual in a shoe box.

She told us that she had a unique system with both her and her husbands laundry. It stayed in a bath full of soap suds and was only taken out when needed. I was not entirely surprised when she said she was the official of the new independent Ukraine who would be travelling with us on occasions to guide us in choosing garments that were suitable for the wealthier Ukrainians. Her only other topic of conversation was always money and on this subject she opened the conversation about 'The Jesus Scroll" and how much was I prepared to pay to see a translation of the Scroll. Her KGB contacts could make it happen and handover the Amulet from the Tomb of Moses.

We parted company at the airport and travelled on to Desenzano to meet our driver.

It would be remiss of me not to mention that in our world wide search for shoes, no shoe and boot manufacturer in the world were the equal of the Italians for quality, style, price and delivery.

Neither Sylvia or myself have ever been communist or entertained communist sympathies, but it was enjoyable to watch the excited expectation of the people of Ukraine, and to help them achieve their goal.

AUTHORS NOTES

A trading partnership between EU Member Countries and Russia is the only way forward to stop a shrinking European Economy.

I am confident that future history books will record Russia's President Putin, as one of the most successful Presidents to rule over that huge Russian Nation. President Putin will be seen as the Russian President who lifted that Great Nation up from its knees after the shock of the economic chaos, caused by his predecessors rushing too quickly headlong into economic and political freedom without having the know-how in place to deal with the gap in the knowledge of how free international trade actually works.

In the space of a few short years President Putin has put Russia firmly back into its seat at the table of the world's most powerful Nations, controlling huge oil and gas resources throughout its sphere of influence, Commodities that will rise in value as world economies recover. Instead of frequently demonising President Putin, member countries of the European Union should wake up to the fact that were they to invite Russia to become a trading partner in the EU, it would open up that vast Country of 500 million people to the economic benefit of both Russia and Europe.

India is not a neighbour. China is not a neighbour to EU countries. The Russians are on our doorstep. A trading partnership with Russia will drag the EU out from a Depression that will otherwise last many years. At the same time encourage all the other former Soviet Countries to become trading partners in the EU, with Russia in its rightful place at the head of the table.

THE JESUS SCROLL TRAVELS FROM JERUSALEM TO KYIV, UKRAINE

Crusader Knights William de Warren and Rayner the Flemming unearthed the Jesus Scroll, during the construction of what are widely known as the "Crusader Steps" leading down to what is said to be the tomb of Holy Mary in Jerusalem, where her remains were put to rest after being removed from the Kedron Valley. Queen Helena, Roman Empress, and Mother of Constantine the Great ordered the transfer. The tomb is beautiful with loving care lavished on the tomb itself; the floor around the tomb and the steps leading down to the tomb is obvious, even to the present day.

The only place in the known world where mixed Asian and middle eastern language scrolls could be translated into a form understood by the Norman French were the Monasteries of Kyiv, Ukraine.

Our early history of that interesting city reveals that Viking raiders travelled down the rivers from Europe towards the Black Sea looking for a place to settle far away from the constant warring in their own lands. These Viking travellers were the true early founders and settlers of the cities of Kyiv and Novgorod. Rurik, a Norseman, became ruler of Kyiv in 850.

Not surprisingly, Crusaders with their Viking/Norman ancestry were always happy to travel to Ukraine where they would enjoy a warm reception from a people ruled over by a Christian Prince who supported the Crusader cause. Many in the local population were also aware of their own Viking roots.

In 988 AD Vladimir, Prince of Kyiv, had been baptised into Christianity. The Roman Emperor of Constantinople acted as his guide and Godfather. Vladimir set up a Monastery for Christian learning in the woods in Kyiv. The Crusaders exchanged the original scroll in payment for the translation, plus their shelter and accommodation at the monastery. The Knights set off on their return journey to England with their valuable scroll and to claim their reward from King Stephen. King Stephen gave the scroll to his trusted religious scholar Roger Clinton on his appointment by the King, to the important position of Bishop of Coventry.

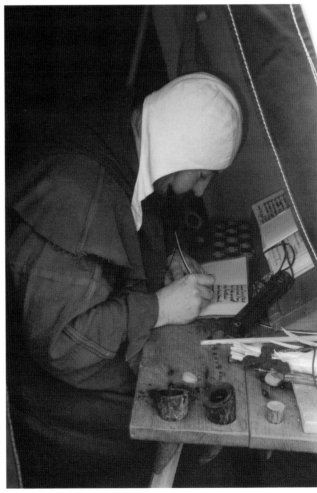

*Monk in Kyiv
monastery
translating the
Jesus Scroll*

THE CIA MAN

The first document, upon which this book draws upon heavily, is "The Jesus Scroll". First featured in my last book, 'The Clintons and the Glastonbury Connection'.

It is a fact that my wife Sylvia and I risked life and limb to gain access to the English translation of the 'Jesus Scroll' translated from a parchment written in ancient French, indicating Crusader origin. The translation was achieved by learned Monks working in a Monastery in a former Soviet Country, known for centuries as the only religious institution in the world where most ancient languages could be understood and translated.

Fortunately, at that time, I still enjoyed good contacts with former senior KGB officers, and ambassadors in that country with whom we had acted in an advisory capacity during discussions to bring about that Country's Independence. The new hierarchy after Independence were indebted to us, because Sylvia and I lived and worked in Hong Kong for a year, setting up supply chains with Hong Kong manufacturers when Russia cut off their supply of essential winter clothing. After which we lived in Verona, Italy, to set up suppliers of shoes and boots.

We also made contact with a Russian who worked with the CIA. Employed by the CIA to track down scientists who had worked in Russia on the design and production of weapons of mass destruction.

Arrangements were made for us to meet Michael in the hotel lounge at Gatwick Airport. We both loved Michael; Russian born, with an American Passport. He was small in stature, but we both knew from experience that he would always place our safety before his own.

Michael was seated at a table close to the pilots' corner of the restaurant in the hotel. After the usual hellos and handshakes, Michael told me that he was anxious that I read the latest version of a manuscript for his proposed book during the flight. I readily agreed, although I knew I had been trapped into a task that would be depressive from the outset.

I edited a previous version of Michael's book in which he talked about the plight of the average Russian living in the Russian countryside; only just surviving the winters on pickled eggs, potatoes, pickled apples and borsch. It was written in a manner that evoked an air of hopelessness surrounding their daily lives with the prediction that the future held nothing better in store for them.

Michael's solution was for the Russian Government to wake up to the fact that, were the government to transfer to every Russian the freehold and title of ownership of the property in which they lived, and grew their food that provided their store for surviving the winter months; Michael firmly believed that such a policy would immediately instill in all Russians a fervour to renovate their properties, improve and trade their land or house in order to better their lot. A happening that would benefit the Russian peoples throughout the whole of Russia. In turn, boosting the Russian economy to an unbelievable level of success and prosperity.

When I asked his views about the likelihood of the Russian Government adopting his ideas, Michael likened the prospects to the story about the Frog and the Scorpion.

THE FROG AND THE SCORPION

A frog was about to swim to the other side of the river, where he could bathe in the sun, when suddenly a friendly Scorpion appeared.
"Please Mr Frog, would you give me a ride on your back across to the other river bank", asked the Scorpion
"Certainly not", the frog replied, "you will sting me"!
"Of course not" replied the Scorpion. "You would die from my sting; and no longer be able to carry me, I would drown".
The frog was uncertain but being kind, gave the Scorpion the benefit of the doubt, and gave him a lift on his back.
Halfway across the river, the Scorpion stung the frog!
"Why did you do that", cried the frog! "We will both die"!
"Sorry" said the Scorpion
"I could not help it, it's in my nature"

THE ARRIVAL IN A FORMER SOVIET COUNTRY

Michael's first task was to get Sylvia and I safely into the former Soviet Country. In a spirit of co-operation, I spent the three hour flight reading Michael's manuscript, after which we were soon comfortable in a five star hotel in that capital city.

Our former KGB contacts had already set up a meeting with a wealthy businessman before our arrival. We were to meet him in a restaurant sited in a forest outside the city centre.

We left our hotel in darkness, and in doing so we were breaking one of our own cardinal rules while staying in that part of the world.

After climbing into the rear of a four-by-four with black windows, the driver announced that he would be circling the town for around twenty minutes or so to shake off any cars that may be tailing us.

When we arrived, we were in for a pleasant surprise, the restaurant was superb with a stage, Russian folk singing and traditional music, plus we were asked into a private room where food was already laid out on a central table. We were greeted by a well dressed business man who looked nervous. Even before we had time to introduce ourselves, he blurted out that the Jesus Scroll was not for sale. He would, however, allow us to copy the English translation because he owed the former KGB officer who set up the meeting, some favours.

He insisted that we tell no one we had seen him, because he was under a death threat, and was in hiding. The business man left the restaurant, ignoring the food on the table, departing in the car that had delivered us there, leaving behind his own well-built bodyguard, who explained pointedly that he was now in charge of the translation, and under no circumstances would we be allowed to retain it.

Sylvia and I were overjoyed. There laying in front of us, at long last, a less than perfect English translation from ancient French of The Jesus Scroll, which we were allowed to copy, word for word, at our leisure whilst nibbling at the food. The bodyguard had already fallen asleep from the effects of constantly sipping Vodka.

Both of us writing at breakneck speed. Shortly before midnight, we released the bodyguard with the scroll. Only then did we realise that, in the excitement that we were left stranded in a restaurant, goodness knows where, without any means of transport to return to our five star hotel.

A large bribe in US dollars to the manager of the restaurant, who was in the process of cleaning and stripping the tables and bar, he agreed to deliver us back to our hotel in his van with me sitting on a blanket on the floor in the back of the van.

Early next morning Sylvia and I were overjoyed. We had a new scripture. In spite of the uncertainty, all the arrangements had worked out like a dream. We decided to celebrate and mark our good fortune by buying some of the beautifully hand painted paper-mache boxes in the local market. Not long into our shopping spree, CIA man Michael, came running down the hill, panting for breath, saying we must return to our hotel immediately. We went with Michael up to our hotel room, straight in the ensuite, turned on all the taps in true James Bond style, and asked Michael what the panic was about. Michael explained that there was some kind of threat to us because we attended a meeting with the businessman in the restaurant and we could be picked up by the Secret Police at any time.

Alarmed, we telephoned our contact in Vienna. He said, "I will arrange to get you both out at first light tomorrow, but stay in the ground floor restaurant, and a young woman will arrive with a bodyguard and make all the arrangements".

Perhaps foolishly, we both became bored with the surroundings in the ground floor restaurant and accepted an invitation from two businessmen, we had not seen for over a year, to eat in the more luxurious restaurant on the top floor. Starting with Sylvia, we each of us in turn ordered from the menu. In conversation about the exodus of Spooks from Cyprus to Vienna, both men looked up as their phones rang at the same time. They answered their phones, stood up together, and with sincere apologies whilst throwing money onto the table, announced that they would have to leave immediately.

Alarmed, and thinking fancifully that it could be a hit, Sylvia and I went to the fire escape and walked down to the restaurant on the ground floor. Not long after we were seated, a beautiful young woman joined us, and explained that a powerful car would be waiting outside the Hotel reception at 6am with bodyguards, who would take us to the airport and get us aboard the first flight to London. We arrived at Gatwick, then home to Essex.

Next day came the bad news. People we knew had been roughed up and arrested by the KGB, and held overnight for questioning. Completely innocent of any wrong doing they were released, and warned not to support or join the up coming Orange Revolution. We had both heard these stories before. Sylvia and I knew that we had to fly to Vienna. Booked into the

Bristol Hotel where we would feel safe, then arrange for our contact, a lawyer in Vienna, to stand by to take us by car on the long and arduous drive, through minor border posts, to bring people out.

All the arrangements were put in place, but as we were leaving the hotel to enjoy lunch in a famous Viennese restaurant, the telephone rang. The caller informed us that everyone was fine. The beautiful young woman who came to our aid in the hotel was on her way to the British Embassy to collect the appropriate papers enabling her to fly to London, Gatwick Airport. Relieved, Sylvia and I checked out from the hotel, and were lucky to obtain seats on the next Austrian Air Flight to Gatwick. After enjoying a cup of coffee, we sat outside Arrivals for an hour. True to the electronic information board, the brave young woman came through the doors in the Arrivals Hall. Surprisingly, quite unperturbed by her experiences, saying 'that is the way of politics in my Country, it can only get better'.

Nevertheless, she was keen to set off with us to our house in Essex where she said she would feel comfortable and secure. The next day the rest of her team flew into Gatwick, a young male Russian speaking computer genius, a female university professor and her bi-lingual secretary. All excited about the up coming election in their Country.

They spent their short time in England getting to know London, improving their English, which in turn enabled us to improve our Russian.

Crossing the Dnieper at Kyiv 1837.
Oil on Canvas by Sternberg, Vasily (1818-1845)

18

THE JESUS SCROLL AND DRUIDISM

Druidism remained very active in Britain, Gaul, and Ireland, even in the face of persecution by the Romans. Druid High Priests were Counsellors to Kings in all those countries, controlling all sacred functions and matters of religion.

Druidism was a pure religion, because its spirituality was based on worshipping one God. The Maggi taught that the soul of man was immortal, and lived on after death in another; reincarnated to the place and position earned by the manner in which a life had been lived before death. Druids taught the necessity of practicing justice and truth, doing harm to no man, cherishing and protecting little children and being manly at all times.

A portrait of a Druid by William Stukeley

Druids held a vast knowledge of natural medicines. They taught divining as a method of foretelling the future, frequently using the techniques of scrying. Druids studied the stars as a reliable method to ascertaining the seasons for sowing and reaping. High Priests practiced casting out devils into animals. They successfully used a herb in the palms of the hands to anoint and heal problems of the eyes. Druids also calmed the winds for herring fishermen with a knotted cord. Druids held regular assemblies where they would rule on disputes and legal matters. Druid Priests required students and followers to be present at Druid Services held in groves in forests where the Priests offered burnt sacrifices at an altar, much in the manner of the Jews.

Britain's orthodox Druid Priests and Arch Druids were the natural forerunners in Britain to the Jerusalem Christians and Disciples of Jesus who arrived at the Isle of Avalon in Britain from AD 38. Druids were easily absorbed into Christian Churches when Rome ordered the extermination of Britain's Druids. This is not the story told by Julius Caesar in his writings.

My reading of history casts Julius Caesar in the roles of Master of Genocide and Invader and Plunderer of the resources of Europe, slaver of countless numbers of women and children of the men murdered by his troops. An idol worshipper, a man in my opinion, on a par with Adolf Hitler.

Caesar's writings about the Druids were largely exaggerations, falsifications, and downright lies. All in an effort to cover up and justify the wide spread Roman practice of genocide. In this case the genocide was being perpetrated upon Britain's Druidic tribes. Plus the vile Roman practice of selling off into slavery the wives and children of the Druids murdered by the Roman soldiers. Only after they had been raped, beaten and abused.

Much of the idolatrous filth in Rome around Julius Caesar supported his policy of wiping out Druids, because they saw the Druid Maggi as a capable leadership, with its own religion, independent and defiant towards the rule of Rome. The selling of the Druid wives and orphans was also very profitable for Rome.

Such was the reputation of Druid learning and integrity, that Kings, rulers, and wealthy families around the known world sent their eldest children to study at Druidic schools. The greatest of these seats of learning in Britain was based at Glastonbury located in the West. The system of study in place in Druid schools lasted for up to fifteen years to qualify for higher positions such as Druid High Priest, and High Priestess.

THE BOY JESUS PREPARED
FOR CORNWALL, ENGLAND

It was this reputation for superior education that led the wealthy Joseph of Arimathea to take his grand nephew the boy Jesus, and his own son Adnam Josephus, at the age of twelve years, to the Glastonbury College of Druidism, where they would gain the best education the world had to offer at that time, and where the boys would be supported and cared for by Joseph's relatives when Joseph was away on his trading vessel.

Joseph and Holy Mary, the parents of Jesus, readily agreed to the plan for the two boys to travel to Britain. The parents motives being the anxiety to get Jesus and Adnam away from Judea where no one was entirely safe from murder, blackmail, or abuse from the occupying Roman filth. Joseph and Holy Mary were comforted by the knowledge that the relatives of the wealthy and influential Joseph of Arimathea would care for the youngsters. Added to which Joseph would be visiting the boys frequently on his regular round trips from Joppa in Judea to Britain, when the boys could exchange letters to their mothers, and family in Judea.

In Judea it was the time of Passover in the Jewish calendar. In preparation for the trip to Britain, Joseph and Holy Mary took Jesus up to the Temple in Jerusalem to ask the Temple Priests for a special blessing for his journey. Joseph of Arimathea, himself a Temple Priest, had taken Jesus regularly to the Temple for religious instruction on special Temple days. It was on those occasions that Joseph and the other Temple priests discovered that Jesus was probably a child genius, and must be afforded the best education the world had to offer.

Jesus was at home in the Temple and stayed at the Temple all day, a place to which he referred as 'God's House'. Jesus also loved the Temple Priests who in return loved him dearly. (The same priests who, in the future, would be calling for his execution). Jesus could barely contain his excitement and tears as he called back to the Priests waving "MY SPECIAL JOURNEY BEGINS, AND MY GOD WILL BE WITH ME ALL THE WAY". The Temple Priests shed tears of love as they saw Jesus running down the Temple steps, trying to catch up to his parents who had scolded him for being too long at the Temple.

When Jesus arrived at his home, he being the eldest, made his farewells to his brothers and sisters, the next eldest being James. Jesus promised to send presents from Britain and letters explaining the way of life there.

Joseph of Arimathea arrived with Adnam to collect Jesus and his belongings. Joseph explained to the whole family that his relatives owned tin smelters near Glastonbury in Britain, and would house and care for the boys. The relatives would teach the boys about mining and smelting, and trading ferrous and non-ferrous metals, essential to the Romans. That the boys would attend the Druid College of Learning and when they returned to Judea, would be wiser and more educated than him, and would be ready to join the family business.

AUTHORS NOTE

On the instructions of Jesus, James, the younger brother of Jesus, headed the Church of Christian Jews in Jerusalem for 30 years following the Crucifixion. James became known as the Bishop of Jerusalem, until he was stoned to death by Romans in AD 62, after hatred had been stirred up against James by the Orthodox Temple Jews who became alarmed at his following and power. James was buried in the Garden of Arimathea.

These historic facts are confirmed in first century scrolls, but omitted from the Bible. It was his brother, James, Jesus instructed to "Build My Church".

Jesus saw the vision that the one God was not the domain of the Jews alone, but that the one God was the God of all Gentiles, and Jews alike. Jesus knew he had the mission to take these messages back to Judea; the Good News for everyone. Jesus knew also that spreading this wondrous news throughout Judea was not possible by one man alone. However, God had given him the wealth to recruit Disciples to build Meeting Houses and devote their lives to spreading God's word. One of the disciples must be a woman to head the women of Galilee.

He knew also that when his mission was accomplished, as a descendant of the line of David, he had to go into Jerusalem when the time was right, and in the manner laid down by the Old Testament Prophets, to claim the spiritual kingdom of the Jews as spiritual King.

Joseph of Arimathea told Jesus that if this is the Mission given to you by God, then I will be with you all the way, but you must know Jesus, that the leader of the Jews in the Temple will bay for your blood. They will never understand that the Kingdom you are claiming is the Spiritual Kingdom of the Jews, and not the power to rule over the Sanhedrin. The Kingdom you are claiming is not of this world

Jesus told Joseph that his Mission is to explain to all mankind that the One God, claimed by the Jews to be The God of the Jews alone, is in fact the God of all mankind. I saw this in a vision as my Mission to spread God's message. The Holy Spirit from the very mind of God will then flow out into the world for the benefit of all mankind, and shall never leave. This spiritual power, direct from God, will wait to be called upon by all who keep God's Commandments. Together with the great gift of eternal life.

THE TIME HAD COME
FIFTEEN YEARS LATER

Years later Jesus and Adnam stood before Joseph, unrecognisable, and beyond doubt Priestly men. Their learning and godliness flowed from them, touching everyone around them. Gentleness and understanding of the human soul. Overflowing with knowledge and secrets unknown to men.

Fifteen years of study and learning was over, it was now time to take this with them, to do good with their powers and spread love among their people.

Adnam
Avalon to Adnam was a Paradise. He chose to stay with his family at Glastonbury, and to continue with his Cor as a teacher, in Paradise.

Jesus
Jesus was compelled to return home to his people. There was much Good News and God's Word to spread. Jesus was aware that the Road he had to take was powerful and dangerous. He felt he had no choice, and yet he had no fear.

Sylvia Rayner

Joseph and Jesus

Leave Britain

for Israel

The Somerset coastline as it probably was in the later pre-historic period. Based upon contour 50 feet above sea level.

Drawn by Eustace Nash

27

Joseph and Jesus Leave Britain's Tin Island to Sail for Israel

L ead ingots from the Mendip Hills were being loaded into the hold of Joseph's ship. Heavy ingots would act as ballast for the return journey to Joppa, Israel. The smaller tin ship from the Isle of Avalon was behind schedule, usually due to sailing against the strong estuary current under full sail to break out from the estuary to the sea to sail round the point to meet up with Joseph's ship in good time to catch high tide. In the meantime a barge had arrived from the inland waterways loaded with ingots of copper, silver, and iron. All to be winched up to the deck of Joseph's ship.

Joseph commented that the ingots were fewer in number than on the usual loading. The barge Master explained that torrential continuous rainfall in the Mendip Hills rendered the cartways to loading points on overflowing rivers impossible to negotiate, resulting in a reduced amount of ore reaching the Jews Houses for smelting.

The ship's Master assured Joseph that no hold would remain empty on the return journey to Joppa because there was a goodly supply of woollen blankets and tents for the Army Storemaster in Rome. There were also many barrels of oil and salted fish, also for Rome. Joseph loaded new wooden barrels for transportation to his fishing fleet in Galilee, to experiment with replacing flat sacks used for storing salted fish from the Galilee which Joseph estimated would not preserve as long as salt fish stored in barrels.

All the cargo was stored and lashed with care, because in the early Spring, while the Atlantic had its perils, the Mediterranean Sea had only just opened and could be very rough.

Joseph looked up from an array of parchments and scrolls he was holding to inform the Master Mariner he was pleased, that for the first time, he had on board a collection of rare skins and furs from North Sea Traders, brought to him overland to Glastonbury by salt merchants. Such skins and furs would be in demand at every Port of call on the route home to Joppa for decorating the clothes of the rich.

Last to be loaded were the live oysters in caskets of brine. A profitable delicacy for Rome, sailed round from Rutupiae to Joseph's ship. Then on to Rome where the oysters would still be alive. The Master reminded Joseph that he had reserved room in the hold into which to load wine during a brief stop in Spain.

Their agent will have collected wine from the vinyards along the Dordogne, Lot and Garonne. The wine would be exchanged for ingots of silver needed by the Spanish Silversmiths.

Joseph instructed the ship's master. Tell the Silversmiths to reserve for me some fine silver goblets which I will collect on my return journey to Britain. Give them extra ingots from which to make fine goblets but keep a careful tally. Ask them also to make a silver scabbard to fit a Roman Sword. It will be my gift to the Storemaster of the Roman Store at Sermioni.

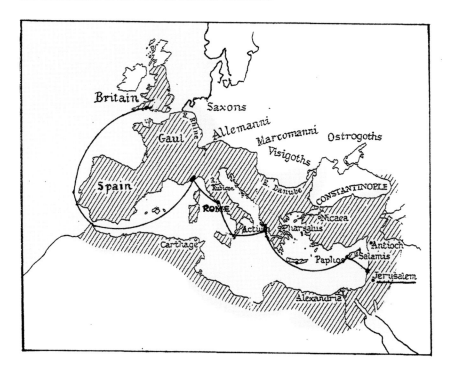

AUTHORS NOTE

Even before the first century AD, the prize possession of a Master Mariner was his magnetic stone, which he kept wrapped in a fine leather cloth. Before setting sail a fine needle of metal would be left overnight on the magnetic stone. The following morning the needle was removed and pushed into a piece of straw. The straw was floated on a small tray of water, where it would always swing to point North without fail. Thus on a dark night or an overcast day, a Master Mariner could always find the North Star.

CONVERSATIONS WITH JESUS

GOD IS GOD TO EVERYONE, NO MATTER WHAT RACE, COLOUR OR CREED.

SAILING FOR SPAIN
CONVERSATIONS WITH JESUS

Standing on the stern of the ship, whilst Joseph was busy checking the tallies, Jesus stared out to the sea and the tin island disappearing into the horizon. Jesus was pondering the fact that life at the Druid Cor was such a life changing experience. Remembering as a small boy sitting on a rock in a Grove of trees staring up at the Druid teacher thinking how impossible it was to try to even imagine spending the next fifteen years at this place. It seemed an eternity.

His thoughts were broken as Joseph rested his firm hand on his shoulder. My son Adnam Josephus is in that horizon Jesus. He remains there, safe from the Roman filth. Part of both of us remains there in the horizon Jesus, but with you beside me I do not feel lonely and sad. I feel excited inside that after all these years, all my plans, all my hopes and wishes, everything is working out. At last we are starting our mission. The road ahead will be painful and hard, but with my wealth we can take a message that will give our people a new hope. A hope that will lift them up from their hardship and despair. Jesus turned and looked at Joseph. "My first message to our people Joseph will be of my vision. That God is not the God of the Jews alone. God is the loving and forgiving Spirit of all mankind. I tell you this Joseph, rich or poor, high or low born, whatever race colour or creed. All men are equal in God's eyes. No man is above another. God is the God of all mankind. No one can put God in a box. No man can gain favour with God by paying money for a burnt offering. No man will gain favour with God making a great show of his religion before men. We must be wary of any group who say we are the way to God. Come with us. Excluding all others. These people are planning to gain power over a man and his money. Many will come with filth and fornication in God's name. The Priests will smile and welcome them and that will be the sign that the end is nigh. For those there will be a special place where they will be smitten and cursed".

"For all that I have learned Joseph, and all that you have seen. Our peoples are so very behind the peoples at our Ports of call". "Yes Jesus, I see enslavement, murder, rape and theft, all consistent with the attitudes of the occupying Roman filth and their evil ways. But this is why our mission is so important. The Romans are the cursed of God. There will be no eternal life for time and eternity for them. There is no hope for them. They will fall and disappear in time. We will go on to be born in another".

Joseph interrupted his conversation to call to the ship's Master. "If the sky is dark at morning, and there is no sun, use the thunderstone needle to keep the ship away from the rocky shore". "Guard it well. We have only one needle to keep the ship safe from peril. This needle has been used since the time of Moses".

THE GRAND PLAN FOR DISCIPLES

Jesus and Joseph both turned to stare at the horizon.

"Your message Jesus, the Good News for all mankind, must be taken to everyone who will listen, not only in our homeland, but to all our Ports of call.

It will be impossible for one man to carry out such a task alone. I have money Jesus, and this is my grand plan. My fishermen on the Galilee are for the most part, the men who minister and run the meeting houses around the lake. They will be your Disciples to travel with you throughout Galilee and down to Judea spreading the Good News, healing the sick and helping the poor. When that task is complete, your Disciples can travel on my ship to all our Ports of business. Taking the Good News to all those who will listen". "Joseph you are my maker. I pray that I am up to the task".

Strolling together to settle for a night's sleep, Joseph said to Jesus, "Tell me Jesus, to what use did the Druids put my gift of twelve precious stones" Jesus replied. "Unlike the Jewish High Priests Joseph, who wore them in a woven pad tied around their chests, the Druids asked the Jews Houses to set the stones in a solid beaten gold plate, made in the shape of the new moon. This was held around the neck of the Druid High Priest with a gold chain".

"What are your thoughts about my son Adnam Josephus staying on the tin island after his appointment as High Priest to the King?"

"It is a grave loss to you Joseph, now Adnam is not entering your shipping and trading business. Adnam is a gentle and loving soul Joseph. Your blessing is that Adnam will be very close to the King. He will be able to watch over and safeguard your extensive interests in the metals and trading business, which will be a blessing if we have to flee from the Romans with the Disciples to Britain, and the Tin Island".

EVOLUTION OF DIFFERENT NATIONS

"It seems to me Jesus that over the period when Moses was leading our people from Egypt into the promised land, the peoples of this Tin Island (Britain) were mining, smelting and casting the tools of great strength which they were shipping together with ingots to other lands. This enabled the people of Britain to farm their land, make cutters for taking the wool from their sheep; shipping pieces of metal to harness and control their horses and mules. Tools for every manner of living, including for the weaving of cloth. Weapons with which to defend themselves.

Do you see that this is the reason why the peoples of Britain are far more advanced in many ways than our own peoples and those of the Ports we visit. Britain is a land where the people do not have to struggle every day for their daily bread. They have the tools and crops and animals around them. They have surplus to their needs. They have store for winter, and food and goods to barter and sell. Animals of burden to carry 'goods' to barter and sell in exchange for luxury goods. Metal weapons with which to defend their families and villages.

These people will grow, advance and develop new things to their advantage. In the lands we visit where peoples toil all day for the days meagre bread. These nations will not advance and develop, or at least their advance will be very slow over time. Whereas those nations with all the advantages; tools, weapons, animals and carriages will enslave the slower, less developed peoples. This has happened in our own lands. We are enslaved to the Roman filth.

How is it Jesus that God gave his message to Moses to lead our people out from Egypt into the promised land using the ancient trade routes to the water holes enabling them to survive and grow in number. What the Jews did not have were the metals from which to make and cast weapons, tools, and harnesses for animals. It was obvious to the Jewish Elders that without these materials, the Jewish peoples would not make the advances necessary to keep our enemies at bay. In their wisdom our Elders sent a colony of Jews to Marseilles and the Tin Island of Britain to learn about these new materials, although our people did not have the wealth to buy their materials in quantities for our homeland. In Galilee we have only crops and fish. Judea has much less than we Galileans. Our nation will always be vulnerable to attack and takeover by others".

ARRIVING AT MARSEILLES

Approaching Marseilles Joseph told Jesus that when they land he would be travelling to Carcassonne to deliver a few goods to relatives. Joseph asked Jesus to stay close to the ship to ensure nothing was unloaded until his return.

DISEMBARKING IN MARSEILLES

Walking along the quayside Jesus felt a tightening in his throat when he became suddenly aware that his friend and companion for fifteen years, Adnam Josephus, was not walking beside him, but was back on the Isle of Avalon. Jesus stopped in his tracks, as he felt an overwhelming urge to flee back to the ship and return to Britain. After a short pause Jesus took a deep breath and felt his panic fade away as he reminded himself that he had a mission to fulfil that could not be avoided. Jesus, nevertheless felt empty and alone. A strange feeling he had not before experienced or felt. Everything around him was just a meaningless noise. Quite different to the happy Port he remembered.

JESUS HEALS A BLIND BOY

At that moment bright, almost blinding sunrays burst through the clouds. Jesus looked down. He felt tugging on his robe. There was a small boy, obviously blind, begging for alms. Jesus crouched down, holding the boy gently by the shoulders. "What is the greatest gift I can give you little man", asked Jesus. The boy replied, "If I could see everything around me from just one eye, I would be a slave to you for the rest of my life". Jesus looked into the boy's eyes. They were badly congested, in need of cleaning away the flies resting on his eyelids. Jesus took an ointment and a cloth from his robe, and proceeded to clean the boy's eyes with the ointment, after which Jesus discarded the cloth and rose slowly to his feet. A great scream issued from the boys mouth. "I CAN SEE. I CAN SEE. What miracle is this, I can see". Alarmed, traders from nearby stalls came running over to the boy.

"How is it you can see?" asked the stall holders. "The Master has cured my blindness. Now I must be his slave for life". "No, not so", replied Jesus. "I tell you this little man. Make this promise to Me. In all your lifetime you will do harm to no man, and that you will give to those that ask. Your promise will be My reward, and the reward of My God that has healed you". The crowd grew around Jesus as the boy told everyone he was cured of his blindness.

Jesus slipped away half walking, half running to the ship. Jesus spoke out loudly to himself "If there was any doubt in My mind about returning to my Homeland, it is gone, for My God has spoken to me this day".

Jesus walked up the gangplank onto the deck, and stood leaning on the balustrade, looking out over the quayside. Jesus could see Joseph in the distance returning from Carcassonne. He was now surrounded by a number of traders. Joseph stopped at the foot of the gangplank and bid his leave of the traders. Joseph stepped off the plank, fixing ropes across so that none could board. Joseph stood beside Jesus. The traders shouted up from the quay. "Allow us to come aboard Joseph and talk to your healer. Let the healer stay with us on shore and share our hospitalities for a while". Joseph waved back and called "I am sorry, but we have to sail on the tide for we have a schedule that we must keep. Others in Rome are waiting delivery of their goods also".

Joseph looked across to Jesus. I heard about the healing of the boy who was blind Jesus. It is a wonderful thing you have done. I was going about God's business Joseph. The blind boy did not deserve to remain in his fate. This afternoon I missed Adnam Josephus. Me too Jesus, for he is my son, but our glory is to allow his will to be done, and not ours.

AUTHORS NOTE

Romans developed an insatiable appetite for Spanish wines from the vineyards on the three rivers in Spain. Wine at that time was nowhere near as strong as it is in modern times. Water was not safe to drink, consequently everyone drank copious quantities of wine which was more like a beer. Distributed into large jugs, oil was poured onto the top of the wine to help in preserving its quality.

CONVERSATIONS WITH JESUS

SPIRITUAL HEALING
PHYSICAL HEALING

CONVERSATIONS WITH JESUS
SPIRITUAL AND PHYSICAL HEALING

"My son Adnam told me Jesus, that you are the most sought after healer in the whole of the Druid Cor. Adnam said that many Druids claim you have performed many miracles of healing. That you healed a man whose eyes were so congested that his sight had left him, and when the man returned to the Cor, bringing with him gold coins you refused to accept the coins. Instead you instructed the man to give the coins to those less fortunate than himself as a token of his gratitude for his healing by the one God.

What secrets have you learned from the Druids Jesus, that have helped you achieve such success as a healer?"

"We were taught an extensive knowledge of ointments and herbal potions with which to treat many different ailments, Great Uncle Joseph. It is to my own astonishment that I remember every remedy for so many physical illnesses. Also those for treating the mind of man, including trance meditation, and the way of casting out devils. Even people harbouring an inner neurotic desire to remain an invalid can be cured through strong spiritual faith. The most stubborn infirmities can be cast out into animals".

"It is necessary for all successful healers to understand the fundamental make-up of a man. The Spirit of man is from God. The physical man is from the animal. Man shares his life with his animal nature. Some men more so than others. Spiritual disorders, whether conscious or below the conscious level result from Sin. The guilty feelings that come from Sin induce illness into the physical body. Sometimes the whole man is ill, requiring both spiritual and physical treatment.

If an illness persists, there have been occasions when I have made an amulet ring of silver, copper, or gold. Engraved flee, flee, and the name of the illness, followed by the words, "God has set me free". A combination of physical, mental and spiritual illness are not uncommon. It is therefore necessary for the healer to have sufficiently charged spiritual power to forge an invisible link between the spiritual and physical realms.

Strength of spirit can heal phobias, fears, lack of confidence, dizziness, fainting and much more. Strong spiritual suggestion should be accompanied by the application of herbal paste or the drinking of an appropriate infusion. There will be many maladies I can cure, and cripples I can heal, when we return to our own lands Joseph".

"That is important Jesus. On my many round trips from Joppa, along the trading centres to Britain; returning to my brother Joachin's house in Joppa four or five times every year I have seen the suffering of the sensitive of spirit. The elderly becoming ill from fear of the cruelty of the Roman soldiers. Other illnesses result from insufficient food when crops are poor or fail altogether. Stress and mental illnesses can result from being unable to make sacrifices at the Temple on feast days due to having no money".

"The healer must exert a powerful spiritual presence, Joseph, so that the patient can know without words the healer is a man of goodness and pure truth. This will forge the invisible, spiritual link. Quietness then engulfs the patient. Further suggestions linked to faith in the power of God and the Holy Spirit, are the substance of confidence and hope for the future. The healing that will take place is not a miracle, but the natural process of nature. It is the achievement of psychic motivation in the patient's subconscious mind that helps in the process of becoming well, because fear and despair are wiped away and the body can work its curative process.

Our Druid teachers taught us that healing of the physical body were best achieved by either the dispensing of herbal infusion, to be drunk as a medicine, or the application of herbal paste to affected parts of the body. Most herbs were grown in the Druid gardens or groves. We were taught to gather herbs by our own efforts. Then followed the processes of infusing by heating water, or grinding herbs into paste and mixing with oils.

Shortly after the treatments had been administered, effort was concentrated from our own physical powers to focus on healing the whole person".

CHOOSE FRIENDS CAREFULLY

"Evil thought and wicked actions can trigger long term illness Joseph. Unfortunately thoughts in an evil mind can be transferred orally to the minds of others. What we learn from this is that we must choose carefully in life those people with whom we choose to associate, and those who we choose to be our friends. We must also guard against what we think, what we see, and what we may hear. No man should envy or admire an evil one for his time will be cloudy and short. They go down to the pit. No man can imagine the terrors they will face. Not for the evil spirit is time and eternity".

SPIRITUAL HEALING

"We teach the patient that God's Spirit is the grace that entices man, but does not compel. Mans failure in his personal life often brings about illnesses, and problems effecting the workings of the body. However, until the man adjusts his life to God's way, spiritual healing cannot take place, whereas a life lived in God's way leads to a mentally balanced, healthier, happier, and longer life. Private prayer and devotion is a way to replenish spiritual energy, and raise mans spirit to a higher plane, where all things are possible. Where both physical and spiritual healing can take place as one.

Our ultimate goal is to become a Son of God, and gain Divine Power. To achieve this we must possess sufficient spiritual energy with which to develop deep spiritual insight. Learning how to achieve spiritual healing in others, is all part of the process.

I encourage families to fix an amulet in the entrance to their homes, with a quotation from the Scriptures of their favourite prophet so that evil will bypass their door.

At each Port of Call on our journey home, I will use my knowledge of herbs to heal those on the quayside at each stop".

"You are truly a great healer and teacher Jesus. By your own efforts you have become a Son of God. Miracles you will perform in God's name".

BE STILL AND KNOW GOD

"Many people with whom I have spoken on my travels outside the Druid Cor, hold within themselves a deep longing to hear of things abnormal or extraordinary, such as the casting of runes for foretelling; the casting down of woods of the stars, and the heavens. Some even yearn to hear of conversations with ghostly spirits, of dead ancestors.

I have seen that some of this phenomena is self deception, unconscious falsification, or trance. Only Prophesy, a true treasure that fulfils the Prophets, is merit. I teach instead that it is better to be still and pray to know The Powers of the Universe, and step inside the knowledge of all things.

To find the truth of guidance in prayer, it is necessary to create a space, exercising patience, to allow the coming together in that space of Prayer and

Holy Spirit. There shall be no evil thoughts, only that which is clean and wholesome and good, within that space. The space will expand over time to slowly fill the whole body, bringing about change and fulfilment as a new inner eye opens to witness the becoming of one with the Sons and Daughters of God. Then the path to eternal life opens ahead with sure stepping stones into a bright future.

It is necessary to work hard in fulfilling our earthly life by following what is honest and good. Only then will the longings and wishes in our prayers be fulfilled. It is within our own hands to make our prayers come good, by remembering that in matters of this earthly world, prayer and meditation are a wise support, but not a substitute for fact".

NO MAN CAN BUY GODS FAVOURS

"For my part Jesus, I will use my wealth to help build more Meeting houses in Galilee and Judea, to bring our new message of hope to our peoples. That God is a loving God. Our God is a forgiving God. That everyone, no matter what wealth, race, colour, or creed, everyone is equal in God's sight. No man is above another. No man can buy God's favours through sacrifice at the Jewish Temple in Jerusalem or by making a great show of his religion before men. This is the message your followers will take to all the peoples at each Port of Call on our journey to our Tin Island in Britain.

Words cannot express to you my great God Son, Jesus, how proud I am in my heart at your success at the Druid Cor. My Son's appointment as High Priest to the King. And your decision to head the Missions in Judea and Galilee. I will not sleep this night for my heart is full of joy.

My Spirit tells me Jesus, that we are together embarking on a great journey that will be remembered through time and eternity, and that your dead father will know of your journey. Others will use your great knowledge and ability Jesus to gain power, authority, position and wealth for themselves. It is the way of man".

AUTHORS NOTE

By the time Jesus reached Joppa his fame went before him the exciting stories of the people he had cured on the journey home.

CONVERSATIONS WITH JESUS

SUPER CONSCIOUSNESS AND MYSTICISM

SAILING TO ROME
CONVERSATIONS WITH JESUS
SUPER CONSCIOUSNESS AND MYSTICISM

Resting comfortably on deck after leaving Port, sailing away from the hustle and bustle noise of loading or offloading, is one of the enjoyable parts of any journey. Particularly when Joseph had achieved his objectives.

Sitting on deck with Jesus, Joseph asked Jesus to explain, what to Joseph has always been a puzzle to him. Enlighten me Jesus, what did the Druid High Priests teach you about Mysticism.

MYSTICISM

"Mysticism Joseph is not a man's opinion. Has nothing to do with the magic or the occult. Is not a confidence trick. Mysticism is an intuitive power dwelling below the threshold of consciousness. To raise mysticism into consciousness, it is necessary for all parts of the mind to work together as one. Mysticism can then be raised above the level of consciousness to a state of super consciousness, a level where the mind is able to know the unknowable.

This results from the unfolding of consciousness of everyday world to reveal the reality of the existence of a higher super consciousness surrounding the everyday world.

Explained as an illuminated vision of the world; all its nature and its future. A mental state that is radically different to normal due to the splendour of its intensity. Also an awareness that the mind is not contained only within the confines of the brain.

There follows a growing awareness of the Divine. Lovable, infinitely capable, obtainable, alive, melting and fusing into awareness of God and Holy Spirit. Imageless, numbingly beautiful. Illuminating a new centre of self, of life, new destiny of self. All no less real than the everyday world. Plus the assurance that life really is eternal.

A Mystic is someone who through simple meditation or transcendental meditation is able to draw all parts of the mind to work together as one, to achieve the mentally altered state of super consciousness that permits emergence of the powerful transcendental self. Personal will and harmony draw close to the Mind of God, to become one with the family of the Sons of God and Daughters of God. Surpassing the plane of day to day reality, even unto supernatural reality. Leading to an awareness that God, as The Holy Spirit, is operating in the world day and night. That life itself is eternal. That the Holy Spirit is the Divine.

A mystic is someone who knows that the Holy Spirit can reside within a Priest in a church, or a devotee following a religion in India, or any man or woman who keeps God's Commandments. They may be sitting in prayer or meditation in a room in their home or anywhere, in any place in the world.

A mystic is someone who knows that the Holy Spirit will flee far from anyone living in sin or fornication of any kind, including any religio living in sin and fornication.

A mystic is aware that anyone entering religion for the purpose of gaining personal adoration, respect, or prestige, substituting their personal vanity in the stead of God, and the Holy Spirit before men, is evil.

A mystic becomes aware that the Holy Spirit is the most powerful force permeating the planet without contravening the natural laws of nature or the laws of the universe.

A mystic is someone who knows that any establishment or group that claims to own or control access to God and the Holy Spirit to the exclusion of every other group may be a force for evil.

After many years of training and practice Joseph, I am able to slip into meditation at any level when I need to refresh my faith by feeling very close to the Divine. But it is not a means of escapism or overcoming reality. One always returns to now, but feeling refreshed, alive and confident in one's own ability to overcome; be a beacon to others. Meditation and prayer cost nothing but they are a safe port in a storm to those who are lost and unhappy or in despair".

AUTHORS NOTE

Transcendental -
Surpassing the natural plane of reality, even supernatural.
Transcendentalism -
System of philosophy that emphasizes intuition as a means of knowledge in search of the devine.
Transcendental Meditation -
Refreshing the mind and body through silent repetition of a mantra.

Sailing for Athens
Conversation with Jesus
Celtic Beliefs
The First Industrial Revolution

"As you are aware Jesus, the Athenians have wealth and independence because they have much silver from their own resources. It will be useful to barter for silver goblets and plates, which are cheaper than in any other Port. We will take what we achieve in barter onto Judea. I will tempt traders into bartering silver in exchange for luxury materials to use in the making of clothing. However, our anchor will be overnight only. We must sail tomorrow to keep to my schedule".

Anchored under the stars, with no swell and a steady breeze, and only the creaking of the ships timbers, Joseph and Jesus were laying completely relaxed seated in two coils of rope taking turns in recognising star patterns, when Joseph asked Jesus. What did your Druid teachers reveal about the beliefs of those living in Britain outside the Druid religion.

Celtic Beliefs

Jesus answered "The tribes believed that there is a domain below ground peopled with Gods and dead tribal ancestors. A supernatural world where their Gods can determine tribal fate relating to crops, animals and the fate of the individual. Dead relatives were buried in a tribal vault. A strict ceremony was followed to erect a stone in memory of the dead. If this process were not followed in detail, it was thought that crops could fail through lack of rain, and tribal members would die of a fever. Follow the ceremony in detail, and crops will flourish. Animals will multiply successfully and yield plenty of milk. The Gods would keep animals free from disease.

Their leaders taught that it was also necessary to keep the Gods in the underground kingdoms happy with gifts, but these gifts had to be new and unused. Gangways walked over flooded areas from where gifts such as new metal tools, or handles, were cast into the water during either the time of the New or Full Moon and all would be well. They named the leading God Janus, who also had a brother".

The First Industrial Revolution

Beyond the Mendip Hills there was a great open pit where the green copper ore was dug. Even children dug into the sides of the pit to free the ore from the soil.

A Shaman Spirit Doll

45

Copper would be brought to the Jews Houses, where smelters would mix copper and tin to make bronze from which they cast tools for all manner of uses. Tools that would be far stronger and more enduring than antlers. Also preferred to tools made from flint. Dug out boats would travel round the coast to meet up with ships from the European trade routes to barter and trade the new strong tools. However, only the Jews Houses were the masters of casting bronze and extracting silver from the lead in the Mendip Hills.

The Druid Priest called this a great revolution. Such was the joy of seeing ore transformed into shining tin or silver, and the casting into tools. Everyone would sing Joseph Is a Tin Man, in praise of Jews and to ensure good luck whilst the process was taking place.

Only the Romans would view these techniques as a gift for making weapons to be used for death, destruction and slavery.

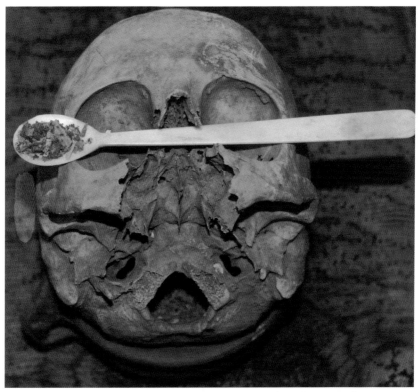

Skull used by Celtic Shaman containing mixtures of powders retrieved with a bone spoon to curse enemies.

" As you know Joseph, we were taught at the Druid Cor to leave drinking water overnight in our silver goblets to rid water of disease. It was also necessary to treat all water to be used in infusions in the same way. Silver water was one of our most popular cures, because it could heal many diseases. The King drank silver water every day to keep himself in good health".

A silver chalice dug up in Cornwall (British Museum). Other ceremonial chalices used were carved from marble on a pole style lathe, soaked in honey then baked to bring out the fine radiant colours in the marble. Some chalices were made using marble cups mounted on a silver base. Imported to Cornwall by Joseph of Arimathea. There is evidence from fragments in historic texts that the Grail Chalices brought to England by St. Joseph were of beaten silver.

AUTHORS NOTE

Long before the first century A.D., Cornwall was known throughout most of Europe, Asia and the Middle East as the pre-eminent area in the known world for the mining and smelting of important metals including tin, copper, lead and silver. Metals, without which, the Romans would have been unable to build up and enjoy their efficient war killing machine. The war machine that enabled them to conquer, devastate, enslave and carry out genocide and ethnic cleansing throughout most of Europe, and part of Asia and the Middle East.

EVOLUTION OF HUMAN SPIRIT OR SOUL

Science has explained to the satisfaction of most thinking people how life on earth is driven by evolution. Eminent Professor Richard Dawkins has written several excellent explanatory books on the subject that should overcome the doubts of most sceptics.

It is my opinion, gleaned from a lifetime of writing and journalism, that alongside the biological evolution of the human mind, there evolved a Spirit or Soul. Whether connected to human genes in the body, or linked to or connected with the mind, I do not know. It is NOT a physical agency, thus it is able to leave body and continue on after death. Phychological condition of individuals, or groups, aside; the difficulty is that it is a phenomenon of which we can only become aware by looking at the way it manifests itself in the psychological and physical worlds. Perhaps meaningful coincidences in time, such as people turning up 'out of the blue' who we may not know, who bring about changes so important to us that they have a material effect on the quality of our lives for a few years or many years. Reflect carefully, thinking back over your life, and I am confident most people will recall such an event, or events, and there is the strong possibility that events are out there in the future. More particularly for people who change the way in which they lead their lives. Everything is possible.

I believe these life changing events are linked to my theory of 'Entanglements in Time', as explained in my books. Entanglements in Time, rely on scientific proof that genes from the past are transmitted from the past, to the present, to the future. Not connected with blind faith, but meaningful science. Unfortunately, although Coincidences in Time, are purposeful and very real, they cannot be proved scientifically, but exist, they do. The good news is that pure spirit, which some interpret as God, is back!

Attracting the Spirit is entirely in everyone's own hands. There is no one deciding that he may have the Spirit, she may not. It matters not who you are; whatever your race colour or creed, whether rich or poor, with or without religious belief; if you lead the life, the Spirit will come.

JESUS ARRIVES
IN ISRAEL

A rriving at the Port of Joppa, Israel, after an absence of fifteen years, Jesus breathed deeply to take in and taste the warm air he knew so well as a child. Jesus commented to Joseph that the temperature in Joppa was so very different to that to which he had become accustomed at the Druid Cor. Air, fresh and stimulating from the lands to the North of Britain, carrying recognisable fragrances from each changing season.

"I have to remember Joseph the teachings of my Druid teachers, not to visit or dwell on the past. The past must be dealt with in order to enable us to move on into the future, with all our wounds healed, remembering only useful knowledge gathered during the past".

Joseph called to Jesus, "The crew have a full load to transfer from the ship to the store this night. The crew will work late and sleep in the store where they will feel secure and happy surrounded by an atmosphere of plenty. Some goods will remain on board for transport up to Capernaum and Tyre. You and I Jesus will travel on with my pack mules and burden bearers to my brother Joachim's house in Arimathea".

"Your Grandparents Joachim and his wife Ann will be thrilled and surprised at your presence. They will not recognise you now you have grown to manhood and filled out with your strength. They can never know or understand what great knowledge and powers you have accumulated over the years at the Druid Cor. My older brother Joachim will scold me for not visiting home on my last hurried visit to Joppa. He may also call me to account for not going up to the Temple to greet the Temple Priests; where both my name and Nicodemus have apparently moved up the list of seniority. A list jealously guarded and squabbled over by the Temple Priests. Let it be so, but I am confident in my own mind that we know so much more about the truth of God and God's ways than all the Temple Priests in their great wheel of hubris. I must remember to keep my conversations guarded Jesus, less I be excluded from the Sanhedrin".

Jesus replied, "The biggest problem we have to overcome in this land Great Uncle Joseph is persuading Jewish Priests that all men are equal in the eyes of God. No one can buy God's favours with the sprinkling of blood from animal sacrifice. God requires all mankind to transcend unevolved primitive ideas and very ancient tribal customs and traditions. Only then will man understand that God is the all powerful Holy Spirit that permeates all men who keep God's Commandments.

I fear Joseph that the Temple Priests with their animal sacrifices, sprinkling of blood and burnt offerings and other rituals performed in their grand robes, is a barrier to their crossing the spiritual bridge from Temple Judaism to the real God and the true Holy Spirit".

FIRST STOP ARIMATHEA

Jesus, Joseph, and their burden bearers arrived at Joseph's home in Arimathea in darkness. Joseph banged on the stout wooden door at the top of a flight of cobbled steps. No response, but heads started to pop out from windows lit by oil lamps. Suddenly there were great shouts of joy as Joseph's brother Joachim appeared at the open door with a large hand held oil lamp. Ann, his wife, stood beside him weeping tears of joy.

"Bring your burden bearers with their loads into the stables where they may sleep this night on the heated pedestal", Joachim called down the steps. "I will prepare food and juice of freshly pressed grapes that everyone may eat and drink their fill. They will sleep soundly on a heated platform with a full stomach on dry land this night". Joachim and Ann both eyed the fine strong upright figure of a handsome man standing erect in silence, behind Joseph.

Both asked in their minds, could this be our Grandson Jesus, so tall and so fine, who had been studying in Britain on the Isle of tin these many years, and has performed many miracles? They both fell silent as tears of joy whelmed up in their eyes. They both hoped and prayed that this fine stranger whose power emanated from his very presence was their Grandson they had heard so much about on Joseph's many return journeys home from Britain.

JESUS MEETS JOACHIM AND ANN

Ann could stand the suspense no longer. "Are you Jesus? Can you be Jesus our Grandson?" Joseph stepped forward. "Ann, God has blessed you both this day", replied Joseph. "This is your Grandson Jesus about whom I told you so much". Ann fell on her knees before Jesus, grabbing his ankles and crying uncontrollably, for reasons neither Joachim nor Joseph could understand. Joachim helped Ann slowly and gently to her feet. "Come Ann, this is no occasion for sorrow and tears. Let us eat and drink together with our guests who have come on such a long and arduous journey to be with us this night".

Laying on their wool mattresses after the celebration Jesus called over to Joseph. "I am yearning Joseph for the views from my home in Nazareth. The view across the valleys to Mt. Carmel. As far as the Jordan Valleys and hill of Gilead. On a clear day I could see the snow covered Mt. Hermon. Below were the olive groves and vinyards. It was an easy journey downhill to the road between Caesarea on the coast, the headquarters of the Roman Legions and only three hours walk to the lake".

As dawn broke Ann greeted Jesus and Joseph with a silver chalice each of goats milk, bread, and goats cheese on a large silver salver. Both men rose and went to the table, Ann seated herself in front of Jesus. Ann gazed intensely at Jesus as he was eating. "I remember Jesus that I was passed the age of conceiving a child, when scrying with his crystal, a Priest from the East who was our guest overnight, announced that I was to give birth to your mother Mary. You are truly a miracle child from a miracle mother. Joseph has told us about your achievements in Britain, Jesus, and the queues of people waiting at the Cor to be healed. We are also very proud that our grandson, Adnam Josephus, has been appointed Arch Druid to King Arviragus. We shall all clearly miss Adnam, but it is for his will to be done not ours".

"Is it possible Jesus that you have returned to save us from the beastial Romans. It is not safe for us to venture out into the market square without Roman soldiers helping themselves to the fruits of our purchases. Even young children, both boys and girls are not safe from molestation by the Roman filth. Please comfort me Jesus, tell me you have come to save us from the Romans". "I have come to save, but not in a way you will yet understand", replied Jesus.

New Life in the Twinkling of an Eye

"Please do not worry so much about your lives Joachim and Ann. When your time is come, you will pass over in the twinkling of an eye to a new life you have earned by the manner in which you have lead your lives here in Jerusalem. You will not even be aware of your passing, and in the life in which you will arrive, you will have no memory of the pain you have endured witnessing the Romans flourish and prosper in spite of their evil ways", said Jesus.

Still influenced by the routine of the Druids at the Druid Cor, Jesus and Joseph rose early to make their way through the sleepy villages with their burden bearers and pack mules. Approaching the City Gates Jesus remarked to Joseph about the large number of Roman soldiers all around. "Do not draw the attention of the Roman soldiers, Jesus. The soldiers will not trouble us because we are on official business". Well dressed and obviously senior Roman figures nodded acknowledgement of Joseph's greetings.

As they walked into the Temple precincts. Jesus called to Joseph. "Why are there tables and money changers in this sacred place. How can this be Joseph?" "Be calm Jesus, much has changed in the past fifteen years since you were here as a boy".

"All the traders at these tables are paying a levy to the Temple. Some even work for the Temple Priests, and share in the profits to be made, which can be very substantial on feast days".

"Come over Jesus. Allow me to introduce you to the Temple Priests". Close by were a group of Priests, clearly deep in discussion about their profits and gains. Full of jollity, they did not notice either Joseph or Jesus watching their every move.

ANGER OF JESUS

Jesus was angry, appealing to Joseph that these Priests, the stewards of God's Temple have allowed the Temple to become a whore, a den of thieves. "I tell you Joseph, when millennium have passed, God has already put in place those who will tear down this Temple, not leaving one stone upon another. I tell you Joseph when millenniums have passed there will arise in Rome another great whore such as this Temple, with Priests wearing expensive gowns, claiming to be God's sons on earth. Outside their precincts parentless children will starve".

ROME WILL DISAPPEAR

"Such will be God's wrath of these vile actions committed in His name by them. The Earth will wrent open and that Temple will be swallowed, and there will be much wailing as we have not yet heard". Let us return to my home early Joseph instructed Jesus, for tomorrow we must travel early to Joppa to ready the ship for our sail to Capernaum.

"You must be excited Jesus, tomorrow we travel to your home in Nazareth to greet your mother Mary and your brothers and sisters. They will be eagerly awaiting their presents and gifts. While we sojourn at your home the burden bearers can deliver the new nets we have brought for my fishermen. They can then pay for some pack mules and travel to Mary Magdalene to collect the salted fish and one piece garments Mary has been storing at her home. The burden bearers may then hand over the last of the orders to Mary's ferry to deliver to the villages around the lake and collect payment".

Jesus told Joseph that he was eager to meet with Mary Magdalene to hear the latest news from the Meeting Houses around the Galilee. "We must place Mary Magdalene in charge of the women of the Meeting Houses round the Galilee. We must also arrange for the construction of a Meeting House for Mary in Magdala".

"I have never ceased to amaze at the wondrous ability of my father Joseph. All our close families are fellahs the farmers; my father Joseph was as you know, the best builder in the district. Capable of building and making in wood and stone: to raise even the largest dwellings in a short space of time. Always he built stone steps to the roof so no one would be caught by fire".

"I long for the one piece cloaks Jesus; in each colour, red, blue, and purple, for which the women of Galilee are famous. There is not a cloak more comfortable to wear sleeping outside under the stars or when travelling", said Joseph.

"Why was the Great Temple built in Judea Joseph? When I hear a wind instrument, I picture the Sea of Galilee shaped like a harp and surrounded by fertile plains; valleys with crops growing on terraces. Olive groves, vineyards, and pasture for the animals. Surely Joseph the land of Adam. Galilee is always so busy, criss-crossed as it is with caravans of burden. Camels, laden donkeys and pack mules, carrying barrels of salted fish, dried fruits, corn, olive oil, unfermented wine, wool dyed or plain in colour. Glass, silver chalices, and all manner of spices and incense.

By comparison Judea is a road to nowhere. Comprising mountainous deserts, narrow rain starved valleys with poor quality cracked and dry soil. If it were not for the olive and grape orchards, the people would face great hardship. Most trade routes also pass by Judea along the coastal routes. The roads to the Temple pass along nothing more than dry dusty roads through the farms and villages where people are really struggling to have sufficient food to eat. Joseph told Jesus that the people are kept poor by Roman Taxes. Every day they have to worry about their daily bread.

"The Temple Vaults are busting with gold, silver, and preserved foods, whilst these people have nothing. These people long for a Messiah to come and save them from the Romans and the double taxation on what little they earn, Jesus".

After the experience of seeing for himself that the Temple in Jerusalem had been turned into a place of grandeur and profit centre, while the people of the villages all around were sometimes close to starvation, Jesus felt a relief boarding the ship to sail to the Port of Tyre, where he could put the memory behind him, at least for a while, of unhappy starving people.

Laying on deck under the stars, Jesus could not sleep for the tension of the excitement he felt inside; seeing his mother after so many years. How his three brothers and two sisters will have grown into adulthood. The passing of his father. Jesus was not sad. His father appeared on the ship and said his goodbye. Jesus knew his father was going on to a wonderful life he had earned by his fruitful life and love of God. His father would have no memory of his past life, but he was going on to a lifetime of joy and happiness that had been hard earned.

Jesus called out to Joseph "we must also ask Mary to arrange to gather together her many followers to hear My address. I will appoint Mary as my first Disciple before the crowd. Then I will address the crowd and tell them of God's plan. However, before that address I will need to recruit Disciples". Joseph replied in an authoritative voice. "Do not be anxious Jesus. I own the fishing fleet on the Galilee, as you are aware. I will instruct my men that those amongst them who choose to go with you on your mission, may do so on full pay, for as long as it takes to expand the Meeting Houses from the Galilee to Judea. God has provided for all your needs".

Joseph could hear Jesus continue in his restlessness twisting and turning. Joseph called across "If you are awake Jesus tell me what the Druids taught you of our one God".

THERE IS A GOD

God expresses presence as a formless energy, known to us as the Holy Spirit. Forever unfolding by coming into existence for some. Always absent from existence for others. Both in and out of existence for the great many.

For those aware of mortality and judgement, the Holy Spirit comes into consciousness, giving life meaning, shape, guidance and healing; spiritual vision of eternity. The vision that resolves all the future into the most advantageous future for the faithful, through portals not thought to exist. Holy Spirit. Its spiritual meaning does not come into existence for the many sinners. For them, only repentance will open the portals to eternal life.

AUTHORS NOTE

Double Taxation arose because of religious and civil demands. The Temple Priests were kept in luxury. Every male Jew over twelve paid a half shekel in Temple Tribute. A tithe had to be paid on crops. Added to which at Temple Festivals there were meat offerings, sin offerings etc., etc. In the cities there was a Poll Tax, Road Tax, City Tax, Water Tax and other taxes.

JESUS GREETS
MARY MAGDALENE

THE TEACHER

Look! That looks funny.

An unusual sight they said
Women floating in a boat on the Sea of Galilee

Can you believe that!

A picnic you say, certainly a gathering of pretty girls
Singing and laughing

Look, one is standing up.
The Blue Lady they call her.
I've seen her before.
Sometimes she is with several fishermen,
Especially one called Jesus the Master.
Her name is Mary she is from Magdala
She supplies boats for the ferry.

She waves to us. The women clap and sing.
What a sight.

You know she is a teacher. They say she says
God is for everyone.

That would be good. We can talk to him
Receive the Holy Spirit.
I think she is in for trouble her and that Master.

Show me the path dear friend, I will follow him!
You had better come too. You are a good honest man.

Sylvia Rayner

JESUS AND JOSEPH HEAD FOR THE GALILEE

As Jesus and Joseph left the Home of Jesus and headed for the Galilee, Jesus waved frantically to his mother and brothers and sisters until they were out of sight. Both men walked and climbed in silence in anticipation of who might be waiting to greet them on their arrival. Joseph had related to Jesus so many good reports about Mary Magdalene, that Jesus was anxious to meet Mary for he barely remembered Mary from his childhood. Jesus and Joseph stopped in their tracks as they rounded a bend in the road and the water of the Galilee came into view. Jesus was surprised to see a crowd of Galileans at the bottom of the footpath. Jesus looked over to Joseph but Joseph said nothing and smiled. As both men neared the gathering, a roar went up accompanied by much clapping and jollity.

A woman stepped forward, peering out from a veil that covered her head. "Welcome home Jesus. Welcome to the Galilee". More clapping ensued. "We have heard so many exciting tales of your miracles of healing on the Tin Island in Britain. Many in the crowd have been waiting since first light. Some have come carrying the sick for you to heal their infirmities and pain".

JESUS GREETS MARY MAGDALENE

"I am Mary Magdalene. I lead the women of the Meeting Houses on the Galilee. My family are part owners and run the ferry and conduct your Godfather Joseph's business in these parts. I have been visiting your Mother Mary with women from the Meeting Houses to comfort and help her after the death of your father. Such a wonderful man, and a great loss to these parts. We, all of us, have been eagerly awaiting your return for Joseph told us the time was near. Joseph has been our Storyteller on each return trip. So wonderful and masterful were his tales of the miracles and wonders you have performed on the Tin Islands. The crowds have grown to the extent that many at the back of the crowd could barely hear Joseph's voice".

Jesus became aware in his mind that Joseph had arranged this welcoming party. Jesus also realised that his family had followed them to the Galilee at a distance not to spoil Joseph's surprise. Mary his mother and his sisters came up behind Jesus and gave him a hug. Mary called out, "This is my Son of whom I am well pleased, but no mother should love one of her children above another". Joseph called over to Mary Magdalene, "Allow me to first run over the business to the gathering, so that we may hear from Jesus, and then commence our celebrations".

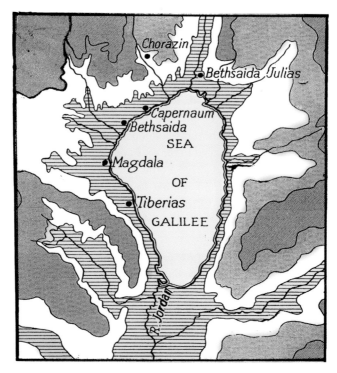

The onion domed Russian Orthadox Church of Mary Magdalene
on the Mount of Olives in Jerusalem

The coming Rapture

PLEASE MARRY MARY MAGDALENE

Mary went up to Jesus. Jesus could see that his Mother had tears of joy on her face. He gently placed his hands over hers. She looked up into his eyes. "Will you marry Mary Magdalene My Son. Please marry Mary, for she is your promised, your betrothed. Everyone living in Nazareth and Galilee, in the hills around would come to celebrate such a magnificent occasion. Please hear my words Jesus. Your father, my husband is gone. I need you and Mary here with Me to carry on our seed".

"I hear and understand your words my Mother, and I love you with all my heart, but Mary and I are married to God. There is no greater destiny upon this earth than being married to God. Our destiny is far greater and more important than becoming man and wife in human kind. We have our mission. A mission that will change the destiny of mankind forever. Mary and I are already married in our Souls". "I do not know your words Jesus. I do not understand what you say. Are you but a stranger to Me after so many years at the Druid Cor?"

"Do not cry Mother. Hear My promise. You will understand. You will see Me in greater glory than marriage. You will become changed by this Glory that is coming to you. You cannot see at this time what greatness awaits you. There is a love that transcends all understanding. Greater than the affairs of man. Greater than a mother for her child. The same is My love for God, the Holy Spirit".

"Your faith will save your Soul Jesus, but it will not save you from a Roman Spear". "Our Soul is not our body Mother. This is part of the great mystery I have to unfold with Mary and our Disciples to our people. They must cast off the old and bring in the new. They must give up the thinking of the ages past, and open their Souls to the light. Any evil Roman can kill our body, but they cannot kill our Soul because it is not in our body, or within the physical world. Our Souls will pass on to Time and Eternity".

"I tell you from My heart My Mother. You will feel the Rapture when it comes. You will see Me in Gods Glory. I promise that the Rapture is coming to you My Mother. You will feel the love that is greater than love in humankind".

Joseph stood on the tallest rock. "I have brought to you from the Tin Island new nets to replace the old shabakeh. I am aware that some may not wish to place their trust in a new net. I urge you to use existing nets and the new nets on either side of your vessel. When you have trawled using both nets, you will soon become aware of the superiority of the new nets. However, I will leave the matter to your own judgement. My next request is to start using the barrels I have brought from the Tin Island to store your salted fish, because the fish will store for longer than in the flat sacks".

JOSEPH APPOINTS DISCIPLES

"Please listen carefully to my new plan. Those fishermen amongst you who are from the Meeting Houses and who would like a new life supporting the Missions of Jesus to expand our Meeting Houses, may leave your boats to travel with Jesus, first around the Galilee and then down to Judea. You may recruit brothers or relatives to replace yourselves on your boats. We will support both yourselves and wives who may care to travel with you to cook and sew to support the group. We will provide for everything. All you need to concern yourselves with is the task of doing God's work. Jesus will now address you to explain the plans for a most exciting future for all".

JESUS ADDRESSES THE GALILEANS

Fishermen, brothers and sisters of Galilee. I bring only good news. There is a place in God's Kingdom for everyone, because our one God is a loving God. Our God loves everyone equally, whether rich or poor, high born or low born, whatever race, colour or creed. Everyone is equal in God's sight. No one man is above another. Our God is a forgiving God to those who fall on their knees in prayer and repent their sins and ask God's forgiveness. Those who keep God's Commandments will be surrounded by the Holy Spirit. Those who keep God's Commandments will never die, their spirit shall go on to Eternal Life. In the twinkling of an eye shall they leave their body and pass on to their new life with no recall of the past. This is the good news we shall take to the Meeting Houses on the Galilee. This is the good news we must spread throughout the land. So let us all rejoice and be glad. Let those who choose to follow me be aware that you will leave your nets and become fishers of men. All the Mothers of the Galilee will be your mother. All the women of the Galilee will be your sisters. We will spread this good news throughout the Galilee. Many will come to us. Many will not understand and go on their way. Those who remain will swell our numbers to seventy, when we will go down to Jerusalem where my brother James will build our church in that Holy place that has become a whore and a den of thieves".

When Jesus saw those scribes recording his words in their Greek he called out to them. "You scribes must learn God's words in your heart. You must keep God's words in your mind to govern your actions and your decisions every minute of every day".

"We must show our followers kinship, love, understanding and communion. In the Temple in Jerusalem the High Priests dress in their grand robes, performing ceremony and ritual, believing that a show of grandeur before men will bring them closer to God. In very truth God and the Holy Spirit do not see their grandeur and hear their great performance. God has already put in place those who will destroy the Temple in Jerusalem. There will not be one stone left standing upon another. I tell you this, God is looking for all of us to come together, and enjoying his love, the love of God, by keeping His commandments. Repenting and asking forgiveness for our sins. Sitting in prayer every day in the quiet of our room and place, being aware that the Holy Spirit is with us every minute of every day. Not fearing death because eternal life will be our reward. Feel clean, wholesome and good in body mind and spirit, and your days will be sunny in this land".

"In a millennium, a great whore will grow up in the filth of Rome, who will dress in grand robes with great ritual. Men who will cause murder, death, and suffering in God's name. God's greatest damnation will be for all those who cause death in God's name. No man can imagine the suffering and pain that will be mete out to these evil doers. Their suffering and pain will last for time and eternity. For is it not God's greatest Commandment "Thou shalt not kill". Is this not God's word from the time of Moses, "Thou shalt not kill". Anyone who kills in the name of God, or sends others to murder in the name of God, their's shall be the greatest of all eternal damnations always.

MARY MAGDALENE APPOINTED A DISCIPLE

"Now it is time to announce that Mary Magdalene is appointed my First Disciple before God. Mary will be in charge of the women of the Galilee. There is nothing hidden that shall not be shouted from the highest roof top. I shall address Mary before all of you that you shall be God's witness. Stand before this rock on which I stand Mary that we make our oath before all our brothers and sisters".

"We must remain pure Mary so that our eyes remain singular looking only to God". Mary replied "I will accept your invitation to be your Disciple. I will remain pure Jesus, because I am now married to God". With that the couple embraced in front of the crowd and kissed on the mouth to seal the revelations that came out from their mouths as was the tradition of the day.

All who were watching were overcome with joy. Men and women were crying great tears while dancing, clapping and singing at the same time. Joseph was crying profusely when he stepped forward and laid his hands gently upon their heads. Joseph looked to Heaven. He cried out, "My God, My Daughter of God, My God, My son of God".

JOSEPH ADDRESSES THE GALILEANS

Joseph stepped up onto a rock. The crowd fell silent. Joseph spoke out, "Do not stop your rejoicing, our joy has only just begun. But remember this day. For many of you this is the first day of a long exciting and fearful journey ahead. This day our journey has truly begun". Joseph slipped down from the rock amid much clapping and cheeping, rising from a crowd full of merriment and fun. Joseph wandered off with his right arm around the waist of Jesus and his left arm around the waist of Mary. "Today we have forged a new Meaning and new Revelation before our God. Revelations that will last for Time and Eternity within a story that will be told through time and eternity. You Jesus will remain pure of body and mind like all those who follow you to become the Sons of God. You Mary will remain pure of body and mind, Married only to God. All those who will follow you will become Married to God. Great is this day. Let us rejoice and be glad in it. I love you both, more than any words can convey. There is nothing more worthwhile that has grown up from a seed. Today, we have planted the seeds of Eternal Life. A life that lasts for time and eternity. Many shall be called, but only few will understand this calling and remain to be chosen".

SECRETS OF THE HOLY SPIRIT

Those who keep the Commandments of Moses and do harm to no one will experience mysterious happenings. The Holy Spirit does not send scribes to write letters, but will speak to you through others. Be wary therefore who you choose to be your friends. Always take your rest in peace, that the Holy Spirit may come to you in your dreams. The Holy Spirit will give you a sense of bad people. The Holy Spirit will put those in place who will warn and protect you. The Holy Spirit will put in place those who will help you achieve your dreams.

JOSEPH AND MARY

MAGDELENE ESCAPE

TO MARSEILLES AND

GLASTONBURY

ESCAPE TO MARSEILLES AND AVALON

Any event at the Temple in Jerusalem was very big business. The main thrust of this business was the supply and sale of animals for sacrifice; whose blood would be sprinkled over the Temple Altar. Sacrifices ranged from a large ram to a small caged bird.

The choice of which depended upon the wealth of the Jewish buyer, and how much money they were prepared to spend to buy God's favour. All believing indirectly that God's favours are for sale. (Animal sacrifice and sprinkling of blood had been practiced around Africa for thousands of years).
As tradition, hundreds of doves were supplied from the hills of Magdala.

The Members of the Sanhedrin the Jewish ruling body of the Temple, controlled most of the business being conducted in and around the Temple precincts. Additionally, they controlled and supplied the Money Changers and those selling gold and silver. No money changed hands anywhere near the Temple without senior Members of the Sanhedrin receiving their cut.

Jesus, James and their Disciples preached against animal sacrifice, and against the Temple becoming a bustling market place. The Jewish Leaders at the temple were incensed at the Christian doctrine. No doubt their main concern was the fear that the teachings of the Jewish Christians would affect their income and Temple business.

CAPERNAUM

Joseph's ship anchored at sea off Capernaum, having completed a four month round trip to Britain. As soon as the ship anchored a hooded man rowed out and clambered on board looking for Joseph. Removing his headwear, the man, one of Joseph's fishermen from the Galilee, blurted out in an excited manner that when he was visiting a relative in Caesarea, he heard that an order had been received from Rome to arrest and question (the Romans' name for torture) all the known Christians in the Galilee. The order placed a price on the head of their leader, Mary Magdalene.

Lazarus and Phillip had sailed up from Joppa with Joseph. Both men were hauling up corn, olives, olive oil, wine, frankincense and woven matting. Joseph called down to Lazarus and Phillip, "I want you to leave now for the Galilee. Sail round the lake and warn all the Meeting Houses of the danger. Locate Mary Magdalene. Explain what has happened and bring her and Martha to the ship at nightfall, with as many others who want to leave".

DISCIPLES FLEE TO MARSEILLES AND BRITAIN

Mary Magdalene, Martha, Lazarus and Phillip and the Disciples who ran the Meeting Houses around the Galilee were rowed out from shore and boarded the ship just after first light. Joseph gave the order to cast off immediately, while the Romans were still sleeping. Joseph informed everyone that they would be sailing direct to Marseilles to avoid being overtaken by a fast Roman Galley.

JOSEPH ADDRESSES THE DISCIPLES

With everyone settled on deck enjoying the early morning sunshine, and not a ship in sight, Joseph took the opportunity to explain why Jesus had been arrested. Temple spies reported that at their open air meetings Jesus and his Disciples preached against animal sacrifice, and Money Changers turning the Temple and its precincts into a large bustling market and a den of thieves.

"The Disciples and Jesus were warned by followers that the Temple Priests were hatching a plan to persuade the Roman Governor, that Jesus and His followers were planning to overthrow Roman rule in Judea, and that Jesus and his followers were terrorists who must be tracked down and executed. Also that the Galilee, the area in which the Christians were gathering in strength must not remain a safe haven for these terrorists. I went with Mary, his mother and begged Jesus not to make the journey into Jerusalem on that fateful day. Jesus said he was going to the sacrifice but not in a way that would be understood by the Romans. We pleaded and cried but nothing we said would change his mind".

"Our life task is not to allow the death of Jesus to be in vain. Our mission will continue. I will organise everything from my new home on Britain's Tin Island, under the protection of the King and his army, and with the help of my son. I have the two goblets on which the 'Ritual of Eternal Life' is engraved. Each Disciple has the ritual engraved on his heart, and on his amulet. My traders at every port will provide each Disciple with everything they need. Every Disciple must travel on my ship to the Tin Island to visit the Meeting House I shall build dedicated to my Great Godson Jesus. Each supper we share together on our journey in this ship, we will pass the goblets used at the supper in Jerusalem before the arrest of Jesus. Each supper we will say a prayer to my Godson".

"Each night after supper we will enjoy the 'Ritual of Eternal Life'. We are the keepers of the secret of Eternal Life. A precious secret passed on to us by dear Jesus. Many will look for this secret, but only a few will find".

Mary, Martha and Phillip Reach Narbonne

A pproaching Marseilles and to avoid the attention of any Roman galley, Joseph ordered the Captain to anchor downstream from the main port and opposite the beaches where the passengers would be landing. It would be too dangerous for Mary Magdalene to be seen near the main Port where Roman spies would be eager to claim their reward.

Luck was with them. There was a steady onshore breeze. The plan was for Phillip to take Mary and Martha ashore in the ship's tender, using a small sail, lashed as a fishing boat because a small fishing boat driving up onto a beach using the onshore wind should not attract any attention or interest. When all were aboard the tender, Joseph looked down on the small vessel with no oars, and a small sail looking like a bird's wing. Joseph knew from experience that the small vessel would be sufficient to carry the party to shore and onto the beach close to Narbonne from where they could walk to their friends and relatives at Carcassonne. There they would be safe amongst their neighbours, none of whom had any love for the Roman filth.

Joseph Sets Sail for Glastonbury

P reparing to cast off, Joseph called down to the tender, "Our God will protect you. My Captain will call upon you, and deliver supplies on his next trip". The tender cast off, swinging swiftly with the wind and headed for the shoreline. Joseph felt confident that all was well, and ordered the Captain to make sail for Britain's Glastonbury, where they would all be safe under the protection of the King and the King's substantial army. Joseph was so excited. He would be seeing his son Adnam Josephus. Not as a boy, but as a High Priest to the King. As Joseph reached his cabin he found he was still holding the two silver goblets he had brought with him from Capernaum. The goblet used to pass wine at the supper. The goblet used to prepare the body of Jesus both he and Nicodemus had taken down from the cross. Joseph sat on his bunk and cried uncontrollably. Joseph cried and cried and cried until his face soaked in tears. This crying gave way to sobbing. How am I going to tell Adnam? How am I going to tell Adnam? How am I going to tell Adnam that I did not prevent Jesus going to his death?

Still grasping the goblets and still fully clothed Joseph fell into a merciful sleep. Joseph woke up when the ship lurched. Placing the silver goblets inside his cloak Joseph called out in a loud voice. "I vow to you my God, I will not tire or rest until the Disciples of Jesus have finished their mission".

"This is my promise my God. Do not let me die until my work is done. In Glastonbury I will build the first Christian Meeting House outside Judea and Galilee devoted to my Godson Jesus. In Avalon the Grail will be safe, and the secret of the Grail will rest with me and the Disciples. Joseph drifted off to sleep with the words of the first poem by Jesus ringing in his ears".

FIRST POEM BY JESUS

There is no death
Our Spirit will never die
We will take a step forward in the twinkling of an eye

As we enter our next life all memories are left behind
All gone in an instant of time

Through the portal we shall reap only what we have sown
Unable to lie and place on others responsibility for our sins

The Good shall go on to paths of
righteousness
Sinners will go on to a future far worse
than that from whence they came
Not for the sinner will be the higher plane

But our God is forever
Time and Eternity shall be His name
To reign supreme above all that there is
Send His Holy Spirit to His Faithful on
Earth to
Guide us and Help us and ease our Pain

The only First Century
portrait of Jesus

AUTHORS NOTE

Like Marseilles, I am using Carcassonne as a geographical guide to the home and resting place of Mary Magdalena, where the language of that area was intertwined with Christian Jerusalem.

TAKING CARE OF MARY MAGDALENE

Unable to sleep Joseph went on deck to take in the brisk air as the ship moved north, to find Lazarus already sitting on deck. Joseph pulled over a coil of rope and sat next to him. "I know you are worried Lazarus but Mary Magdalene will be safe with her relatives near Marseilles. My ships call at the Port on each return journey to Joppa. The captains will see to it that Mary has everything she needs. Mary's life will be full. After enjoying the reunion with her relatives, Mary will be busy gathering textiles for our ships. How long it will take to mend her broken heart only our God will know".

"Mary loves Marseilles, and the climate there. She travelled many times by ship to Marseilles with her relatives to collect the fine materials used by the women of Galilee in the making of their one piece garments, sought after by traders in the many Ports we travel. Everything is in place for Mary to continue with all the things she loves.

I fear Lazarus that no Port with a Roman Garrison will be completely safe for me to visit at this time. However, I should be beyond the reach of the Temple assassins. I comfort myself with the thought there is much to do now Jesus has gone. Many of our Roman traders will be more interested in the day to day relationships and profiting from their trading businesses, than obeying the will of their distant masters to report on my whereabouts".

JOSEPH PLANS DISCIPLES MISSIONS

"I cannot predict at this precise moment Lazarus when it will be safe for me to leave the protection of King Aravagus in Britain, but until that time comes, my ships will transport Disciples from Joppa to Avalon, where I will instruct and disperse them to all the main Ports on our trading routes. I will deposit money and supplies with our close contacts at those ports to enable Disciples to sustain and enlarge their missions".

Dawn was breaking. Lazarus rose to his feet, placed his arm around Joseph's shoulder and gave him a hug. "You are my brother in God. I know your heart was broken into a thousand pieces when you and Nicodemus took Jesus' body whipped and bleeding, from the cross with his legs unbroken, and a wound on his side. You still wear the heartbreak on your face and in your eyes, but soon you will be with your son Adnam at Avalon to whom you have to break the sad news. With Adnam around you, feelings will flow back into your heart".

"Comfort yourself Joseph with the thoughts that whilst the Romans think they have completely silenced our missions, they are not aware that we have bigger fish to catch, and because mariners have wings to fly across the seas, everything is possible. In the meantime, James the brother of Jesus, will carry on our mission in Judea in and around Jerusalem".

Joseph rose slowly to his feet, placing his arm around the shoulder of Lazarus. "In Avalon Lazarus, we will all be safe. We will enjoy the protection and hospitality of King Aravagus, and his family. You cannot imagine Lazarus how much you have to see in Avalon and around that is new to your eyes. A world so different to Bethany and Judea, that you will be lost for words for many a day. You will delight in so many Jews houses producing tin and other metals where traders are queuing at their doors to buy the fruits of their labours. When we arrive Lazarus, you will eat and rest and enjoy yourself. This is my promise to you my dearest friend and supporter of my Godson".

FIRST CHURCH OUTSIDE JERUSALEM A.D.38

"When you have rested Lazarus, I will explain my plan to build quickly the first Meeting House outside Jerusalem at Avalon. There we will worship and make plans to carry on our work. Disciples will reach out from all the Ports to which our ships travel from Avalon to Joppa. Our base will be here, but through our Disciples and brothers in God we will reach out from our sailing ships to many peoples in many lands. I have with me Lazarus the two silver chalices we passed around the table at our last supper in Jerusalem. When we meet, the Holy Spirit will be in Him and He will be in us.

I am going to my Garden of Eden Lazarus, to see my son and find solace for my heavy heart. What we have to remember Lazarus above all things is that this is the time for a new beginning. A time when Disciples can spread the Good News at every Port of call. I know Lazarus that I disagreed with Jesus at the manner in which He offered himself up to the slaughter in Jerusalem, but it was for his will to be done, and not my will to be done. We can be with Jesus again in Spirit when we offer the chalices round the table at supper on ship and in our new Meeting House at Glastonbury. Come Lazarus, We are both tired. So much has happened in the past days. Let us take our rest in prayer and sleep for tomorrow is a new beginning. Tomorrow we will be born again. When I have finished God's work, and on the day of my death, all of the chalices of the Holy Grail will be buried with me on my tin isle in my beloved Avalon. The other I shall commit to the care of my son, Adnam Josephus. We will build a new Jerusalem at Avalon".

72

CONCLUSION

CONCLUSION

THOUSANDS OF YEARS OF IMAGINED GODS

For thousands of years in the past and up to a few hundred years ago, mankinds primitive unevolved intellect dreamed up a pantheon of many Gods occupying positions of imagined importance that influenced the affairs of everyday life for every individual. All imagined Gods whose portended powers were thought to be not only influencing the growth of crops, but also good or bad fortune bearing upon almost every aspect of daily human activity. Fanciful ideas and imagining of the human mind embellished over thousands of years by so called priests to reinforce their hold over their followers.

It would take a powerful computer to calculate the almost inestimable time, effort and physical resources, literally thrown away on this absolute nonsense; prayers of gibberish that influenced absolutely nothing, and no one.

Fortunately, the human intellect evolved, and the imagined Gods lost their pretended divinity. The myths surrounding them went through stages of disintegration, descending into a posterity that would no longer give credit to their divinity; they become mythical personages, changing again to the caprices of their euhemerism descending into mere fables. This, for me, brings down the curtain on the history of religion over the first period in human history. And there is no finer example to illustrate the way in which human intellect evolved and developed over time.

FALSE GODS AND IDOLS START TO DISAPPEAR

My second period is ushered in by the Jews. That great Prophet Moses. Jewish or not, everyone loves Moses, the Prophet who led the Jews out from captivity; slaving for the Egyptians. Travelling the long established trade routes and watering holes to their Promised Land. Along the way Moses presented the Jewish peoples with the Ten Commandments. That one single act. The concept of the One God and the Commandments. The revelations on the mountain, driven by the Holy Spirit, that changed the destiny of mankind forever, fetching, rule of laws, civilisation, community and family home. Bringing to a close thousands of years of fanciful imaginings.

Those who most benefited from the reign of imagined Gods over the thousands of years of their imagined existence were the men of weasel words, and the crafty, the Priests. The men who claimed that they, and they alone, were the route of communicating with those Gods. Their lies will have brought them money, power, authority, and an unearned respectability.

CONCLUSION

The closure of the first period of religious history paved the way for Holy Spirit and Eternal Life. All coming together to open what is my second period of the evolution of the religious mind.

EVOLUTION OF ONE TRUE GOD

It was Moses who evolved the concept of one single God ruling over Jewish human kind, but for Moses God was for the Jews alone. Jews claimed that they, the Jewish people, are the chosen race of God. One consequence of this was to raise a sword against all other religions. The great Prophet Moses did not write or teach that the soul is immortal, or give guidance about possible judgement and life after death.

What Moses fetched was incomplete. Moses was incomplete because immortality of the Soul, Endowment of Holy Spirit, Judgement after death all remained in limbo for thousands of years until the great Prophet Jesus exclaimed, "Other sheep I have which are not of the Jewish fold". Jesus explained about the immortality of the Soul, the Holy Spirit, Judgement. All more spiritual than the Mosaic.

THE DRUID RELIGION

I believe that the Druid religion was closer to the concepts of Christianity than the Mosaic. Druidism had but one God. 'YESU' The Druids had a Trinity. The Creator the past, the saviour the present. The Great the future BELI, TARAN, YESU. All bound to the idea of eternal progression of man and the universe. Pure good. Pure happiness. Evil man, fallen man, continually returns until he has reached the required state.

Wickerwork Curch built in AD 38 at Glastonbury by Joseph of Arimathea

CONCLUSION

THE OLD TESTAMENT
A WONDERFUL HISTORY BOOK

The work of archaeologists and the discovery of scrolls in the Middle East have uncovered the reality that many of the stories in the Old Testament are simply not true. What we have for the most part, are carefully woven and embroidered spin, worked on incidents passed on orally or by written tradition, woven in a way to give these incidents supernatural powers to gain authority for their story. Stories that are more fantasy than truth, with the occasional Prophet thrown in for good measure, uttering prophetic foretellings, most of which did not come true. Those that did work were written after the events.

Viewed in the cold light of analysis, the Old Testament does not confirm that the Jews are the chosen race of God. In reality their religion was incomplete. How could they be the chosen race. We are all fully aware that God cannot be bought with burnt offerings, the sprinkling of blood, or a grand show of religion before men, even in the finest robes backed up with gold and silver paraphernalia.

Nevertheless the Old Testament is a wonderful, wonderful, history book. Absolutely full of wisdom and advice as relevant today as it was at the times at which it was written: Thousands of years in the past. Who would want to be without the Old Testament.

NEW TESTAMENT SPIN

The oldest known manuscript, copies of the bible, do not date back before the early centuries of the Christian era. The oldest is a Greek copy at the Vatican in Rome, dating back to the fourth century AD. The oldest fragments, the Gospel of John, dates to AD80.

It is to me a source of fascination that scrolls unearthed in the last sixty years, and recent archaeological discoveries, reveal that whilst confirming the historic reality of the existence of the Prophet Jesus, most of the stories in the New Testament woven around Jesus are simply not true, but beautiful tales spun on gleanings and sayings about a special breed of men. The stories were spun and dressed up to give pretend supernatural authority to gain control, money, respect and power to the modern Church, who went even further, creating their own deities. Church authorities taught that through their Priests alone, was the only way to God. Further enforcing power and control over their followers.

CONCLUSION

THE TRUTH OF GODS HOLY SPIRIT EMERGES
AND IGNORANCE AND DOGMA FALL AWAY

Only now, in this age, in these times, freed from the blind ignorance of unevolved mind, can we begin to see the truth of reality, as it really is. Now we stand in the light. We can see those who try to gain control over us by claiming if we do not go to them and follow their rigid ways, we will go down to hell and damnation. They are more in need of our guidance than we are of theirs. They cannot see that the Gods have fallen off their throne in the sky. We on the other hand are free. We have freedom to choose between paths of good or evil, and by our choices we will be judged.

MAN WILL BECOME CYBORG MAN

Any evil choices we make, the consequences will be visited on our children, and our own life.

We have reached the point in the physiology of man where the heart will be unable to feed a larger brain than man possesses at the present time, say some research scientists. Fortunately, all is not lost for the future of mankind, because computers, not requiring any increase in the body's blood supply, will fill the need for the continued development of the capacity of the human brain to ensure mans survival. Giving the brain greater unimaginable capability. Ensuring the survival of mankind during the coming Mass Extinction events.

Looking at such a development from another point of view. Is it not amazing that man and the development of Cyborg Man, were entangled in time to work out the survival of humankind. Tiny links will be embedded in mans head that will link the brain to unimagined powerful computer capacity. A capability that will enable a section of mankind to survive mass extinction.

I have strived to unveil what history reveals over thousands of years. A step by step change in the evolution of the thinking capacity of the human mind, weeding out all that is a nonsense along the way.

CONCLUSION

THE HOLY SPIRIT AND ETERNAL LIFE

I now merge the sections together, to give my treatment of the most important elements. The Holy Spirit and Eternal Life.

My own personal conclusions are not based on blind faith. I have enjoyed rare prophetic visions myself and prophetic dreams about events that have come true. What I do know without any doubt is that there must be what I can only describe as an external agency that does come into our time and space, triggering visions or prophetic dreams. The same external agency that drove Moses to give the Ten Commandments that changed the destiny for the Jewish peoples, bringing civilisation, society, community, and home. The same external agency that drove the Prophet Jesus to drive the message that God and the Holy Spirit were for all mankind. No matter what race colour or creed. High born or low born. Everyone is equal in Gods eyes, everyone has access direct to God and the Holy Spirit through prayer, and access to Eternal Life by the way they lead their lives.

I firmly believe that the External Agency that came to people in our time and space is the Holy Spirit. I know of no stronger pointers to there being a divine power and purpose in life, and a purpose for the existence of the universe. So there is hope for literally every man and woman on the planet, and that hope does not cost any money. Just a few minutes of prayer in a quiet place and thinking before we speak and act, can transform personality and lives.

CONCLUSION

ANGELS, VISIONS AND DEMONS

VISIONS

The only person I met personally who related to me a vision that I absolutely believe, is Sister Katerina, a Nun who attended the Altar of Crucifixion in the Holy Sepulchre, Jerusalem. Who told her story to camera in my Documentary Jerusalem.

EXTRACT FROM THE AUTHORS BOOK
THE CLINTONS AND THE GLASTONBURY CONNECTION

SISTER KATARINA'S MIRACLE

My wife and I were staying in Jerusalem for the purpose of making a documentary to illustrate the important principal to both children and adults alike that Christians, Muslims and Jews have a God given right to follow their own beliefs without fear or favour and must learn to live in harmony and to respect each other's differences.

At first we found it difficult to obtain permission from the various church authorities to film at the locations we had chosen and scripted. Permission to film Mary's Tomb, and the steps built by the Crusader Knights leading down to the Tomb where the Crusaders uncovered the 'Jesus Scroll', proved difficult. Equally problematic was gaining a licence to film within the Holy Sepulchre itself built over Calvary. However our dogged determination won through, we filmed in both locations in the early hours.

We felt very privileged as we entered the Holy Sepulchre at six a.m. with our film crew. Our first pleasant surprise was to be greeted by a serene and seemingly elderly nun Sister Katarina, standing opposite the Altar of Crucifixion; her dark robe and beautiful ageless eyes lit only by candlelight; she looked like an Angel.

The huge domed building was cold in the early morning. We sat warming Katarina's hands whilst at the same time inviting Katarina to talk to camera about the process of being chosen to serve at what most nuns would regard as the most holy place on earth.

CONCLUSION

Katarina opened to camera describing her vision:

" I was very ill lying in Miami Florida, and thought to be dying, when I had a vision of Holy Mary who told me that I would not die, but would serve God in Jerusalem. Then I saw a vision of the Old City of Jerusalem after which I made a miraculous recovery from my illness, and was transferred to Jerusalem, where I serve God every day".

I asked Katarina if I could have a button from her cardigan or coat, as it would be a special blessing to have a memento from someone so loved by God as to be chosen to receive such a vision, and to be sent on such a special mission. Katarina replied to my utter astonishment, "I have been waiting for you. I have the white stone for you. You will read the Urim and Thummin".

Katarina explained that the white stone was a piece of Calvary that came away in her hand when she was cleaning the top of Calvary in preparation for a bullet proof glass cover to be fitted over the point where the true cross entered the natural rock.

Sylvia and I returned home to England to cut and edit seven hours of film to a programme length of forty minutes. When that important film was finished, we set about looking for a Urim and Thummin.

The next vision was one of my own. My brother, who is 18 months older died about four years ago. I loved my brother and remember the sadness and aching heart, and tears, as I stood in my garden singing his favourite hymn to the setting sun and saying goodbye.

One night recently I sat upright in bed when my brother appeared in my room, shortly after I had written about entanglements in time with our ancestors. My brother appeared smartly dressed in a pinstriped suit, and spoke to me with a message. I thrust out my hand to shake his, but there was nothing there. I blurted out that I loved him and missed him, and the vision faded. I stayed awake because I was annoyed with myself for not listening carefully to what he said. I could, of course, have been asleep all along and dreamed the whole event, but I don't think so.

CONCLUSION
THE HOLY SPIRIT

I have read many accounts of people claiming to see visions, and I now believe that it is a phenomena that is real. However, this conclusion now raises the question in my own mind. What is the agency that produces these visions. Leaving aside drug addicts and drunkenness, it is not something which is common. More properly described as rare indeed. Real meaningful visions appear to be supernatural. The only agency I can bring to bear on this phenomena is the Holy Spirit.

AUTHOR'S PHOTOGRAPH OF THE ALTAR OF CRUCIFIXION
IN THE HOLY SEPULCHRE IN JERUSALEM
TENDED BY SISTER KATARINA

CONCLUSION

The Holy Spirit does not communicate by letter or e-mail so far as I am aware. Perhaps the Holy Spirit triggers activity in the brain that triggers a vision to communicate a message. What is difficult to separate, is that people who have a strong belief, see that belief all around them in everything they see. Previous to that I had a prophetic dream about building a Church. I helped build that Church. Now I write from personal experience of a prophetic dream that became a reality.

THE CRUSADER STEPS AND FLOOR LEADING
TO HOLY MARY'S TOMB IN JERUSALEM
WHERE THE AUTHORS ANCESTOR CRUSADER KNIGHT
RAYNER THE FLEMMING DISCOVERED THE JESUS SCROLL
MOTHER AND FATHER ANN AND JOACHIM
ARE BURIED ON THE LEFT AND RIGHT OF THE STEPS

CONCLUSION

My own revelation gained from the insight of writing books and film-making, is the realisation that the religion Jesus took back to his home country Israel when he returned from the Druid Cor. Christianity, did not emerge entirely from the Jewish Mosaic Law, as everyone has been taught over many centuries. What Jesus taught came from the Druidic Religion that in turn came down from the Chaldeans in Babylon. This realization, from historic facts, sets all Christians free from Judaism and the Mosaic Law, and the same consideration applies to all other religions.

The Jewish Law given by Moses was not complete because it did not contain Immortality, "Life after Death". Only the Chaldean and Druid Laws taught by Jesus gave Holy Spirit and Eternal Life. The full and complete revelation for the whole of mankind. Absolutely separate from Judaism and the Mosaic Law. A gift to every man, woman and child and religion on the planet. AND ABSOLUTELY FREE.

INTELLIGENT DESIGN AND PURPOSE FOR LIFE ON PLANET EARTH

All the scientists on planet Earth have been unable to create viable life, as we know it, from non living inorganic matter. Nevertheless, when life came into existence, life has continued to progress over time by a constant process of evolution.

It does not require a great leap of genius to realise that although life followed a course that may be explained by Darwinism, life itself probably did not originate or could not have originated on this planet. However, to remain consistent we must continue to search for the origin of life, even if it means looking out into the universe.

My starting point in looking for the clues is the realisation that human life generates the future. I explain this point in my book 'The Clintons and the Glastonbury Connection'.

CONCLUSION

EXTRACT FROM THE AUTHORS BOOK
THE CLINTONS AND THE GLASTONBURY CONNECTION
ENTANGLEMENTS IN TIME

INTRODUCTION

Anyone who doubts that there is a connection through the loop of time in our local universe linking the past to the future and a feedback in the loop of time connecting the future to the present, should consider the events that unfold in this book.

If you have ever looked into a mirror in a moment of quiet and wondered whom it is staring back, the answer is deeper than you may think. The person you see in the mirror is only part of the story of the person staring back. There are hundreds of other generations of people who have contributed to the DNA and genes within the person reflected in the mirror. Distant relatives who you will certainly never meet and you may never ever learn of their existence, but exist they did, and they continue to live on in your genes.

Most people will know about the life of their parents or grand parents, or even their great grand parents, but what about the individuals before them; The distant relative who passed on their DNA to them and you. What was their place in their society? What did they have to do to survive in their lifetime, what was their story? Were they even living in the same country? Which part of their genes have you inherited? What inherited traits from your ancestors live on in you and are they genes to die for? If your name is Clinton, Bush or Washington, you certainly have inherited genes to die for!

DNA is a nucleic acid that is the main constituent of all organisms on the planet. DNA is self-replicating and plays a central role in the transmission of hereditary characteristics from parent to offspring. Your DNA records where you came from thousands of years in the past, and is your passport through time.

The structure of DNA molecules takes the form of a double helix – two strands coiled around each other. During replication the strands of the helix separate, producing identical copies of the original helix – accurate self-replication.

CONCLUSION

An expert working in a laboratory can extract DNA from bones and other body parts many thousands of years old with the qualification that the remains have been preserved in conditions that have enabled DNA to survive. Once extracted, DNA from ancient body parts (or body fluids) can be compared with the DNA of people living today. One of the uses of this information is to provide a pointer for people living today to where the area or region their ancestors originated.

At death any individual is not discarded because Genes live on in their offspring or shared genes in their blood relatives live on into the future. Indeed, human life generates the future, and remains inextricably linked to the loop of time and the past.

SECRET OF ETERNAL LIFE

We exist by courtesy of our dead ancestors
The future exists by courtesy of present day humans
This is the secret of eternal life.

It appears that everything exists by courtesy of everything else. If this explanation is not clearly a meaning and a purpose for life, then I fail to see what is.

The only purpose of the past is to generate the future, and the future flows on from the past towards infinity. All made possible by everything existing by courtesy of everything else. Intelligent purpose, intelligent design from an intelligence existing outside the planet somewhere in the universe.

God is back! It follows that intelligent people will realise that man has a moral responsibility, even imperative, to usher the best man can be into the future. Of that I am certain.

The other form of life upon which humankind is entirely dependent is the planet on which we live, is itself a living cell with intelligent purpose that does its own thing without regard to whether human beings are in the vicinity of a force that may be taking place such as volcanic explosion, or earthquake. I explain this in my book, 'The Clintons and the Glastonbury Connection'.

CONCLUSION

MASS EXTINCTION IS ON ITS WAY

Mankind is damaging, destroying and poisoning the fabric of planet Earth. Plus upsetting the balance of everything that is existing for everything else on the planet. Upsetting this balance has triggered the onset of changes that will rid the planet of the problems. After which the planet, by induction, volcanic activity, and earthquakes, renew its fabric.

Mans extinction is on its way. The few that survive will be the new cyborg man, with the ability to call upon unimaginable computer power by thoughts alone to show mankind how to rebuild from a small base, making human beings great again without making the mistakes of the past.

I propose to show entanglements in time at work by reaching back nearly 2,000 years through time to continue the second part of my story, a history based on actual historical facts known to few people outside the Vatican Library. Information brought to light by the discovery of The Jesus Scroll, written by Joseph of Arimathea, Grand Uncle of Jesus, who was at the heart of the very first Industrial Revolution in world history. Developments that evolved in Cornwall, England, in the first century AD. Embracing Ireland, Wales, and many other countries to make England, the first capital of non-ferrous metals in the known world. This important history and story has remained hidden through careful manipulation by the Catholic Church.

Postcard Dated 1905, Glastonbury Abbey Reconstructed

A rough cast bronze cross, believed to have been worn by St. Augustine a Catholic Missionary sent to England about 597AD many years after the first Christian Church built by Joseph of Arimathea and the disciples of Jesus at Glastonbury

TWO SOURCES OF RESEARCH

SHOWING INDISPUTABLE PROOF

FROM HISTORIC TEXTS

REVEALING BOTH THE

EXISTENCE OF JOSEPH OF

ARIMATHEA

AND HIS LIFE IN ENGLAND

ESTABLISHING THE FIRST

CHRISTIAN CHURCH IN

AD 38 AT GLASTONBURY

THE VOYAGES OF

JOSEPH OF AVALON

IMPORTANCE TO HISTORY OF THE RESEARCH BY
THE REV. R. W. MORGAN IN 1860

My own research path through history co-joins the story in my previous book about the Jesus Scroll that tells us of the arrival of Jesus at Glastonbury in AD14. Jesus travelled to Cornwall (with his cousin Adnam Josephus) and Joseph, his Grand Uncle, Joseph of Arimathea, to start 15 years of education and training by the Druids at Glastonbury.

My story fits snugly together with the research path and book by Rev. R. W. Morgan confirming beyond doubt, using different historic texts from around the world, the return of Joseph of Arimathea to Glastonbury in AD 38, seeking refuge with his extended family in Cornwall after his expulsion from Judea by the mad Roman Emperor. Not long after his arrival in Cornwall, Joseph went on to build the very first Christian Church outside Jerusalem, at Glastonbury in AD 38. The extensive and comprehensive research by the Rev. Morgan confirms the story beyond any shadow of doubt, the establishment of the very first Christian Church in the world, established in Britain in AD 38, visited by Disciples, all centuries before any missionary or monk arrived from Rome or elsewhere on the shores of any part of Britain.

CONCLUSION.

FROM the preceding investigation ensue the following conclusions : —

1. Before Christianity originated in Judæa, there had existed from the remotest period in Britain a religion known as the Druidic, of which the two leading doctrines were identical with those of Christianity, viz., the immortality of the soul and vicarious atonement.

2. That this identity pointed out Britain as of all Gentile countries the one best prepared for the reception of Christianity.

3. That the only religions persecuted by the Roman government were the Druidic and the Christian.

4. That this common persecution by the great military empire with which Britain was engaged in incessant hostilities from A.D. 43 to A.D. 118, materially aided in pre-disposing the British mind in favour of Christianity.

5. That Britain, being the only free state of Europe, was the only country which afforded a

---

4 Bede was a very earnest adherent of the novel papal Church, introduced A.D. 596, by Augustine into Britain, but the honesty and simplicity of his character has rendered his history in many respects a very inconvenient and abnoxious record to the said Church. What became of the remains of St. Peter and St. Paul? At Rome they still pretend to exhibit them, but Bede—and it must be remembered he is a canonized saint in the Roman calendar—expressly states that the remains of the bodies of the apostles Peter and Paul, the martyrs St. Lawrence, St. John, St. Gregory, and St. Pancras, were, at the solicitation of King Oswy to Pope Vitalian, removed from Rome to England, and deposited at Canterbury A.D. 656, Pope Vitalian's letter to Oswy being extant.—(Bedæ Hist., lib. iii. c. 29.) Their remains, then, if any, repose in British soil.

secure asylum to the Christians persecuted by the Roman government.

6. That a current of Christianity flowed into Britain from the East contemporaneously with the first dispersion of the Church at Jerusalem, A.D. 35—38.

7. That the first planters of the Gospel in Britain never were in Rome at all, but came hither from the mother Church at Jerusalem.

8. That these first planters were Joseph of Arimathæa and his associates, who settled under the protection of the British king Arviragus, in the Isle of Avàlon, Glastonbury,—one of the Druidic cors of Somerset.

9. That among the earliest converts of Joseph and his fraternity were Gladys (Pomponia Græcina) the sister, Gladys or Claudia, and Eurgain, the daughters, and Linus the son of Caractacus, prince of Siluria, and military dictator of the national forces against the Romans.

10. That the second planter of the word was Simon Zelotes the apostle, who was martyred and buried in the Roman province, probably near Caistor, in Lincolnshire.

11. That the third planter was Aristobulus, one of the seventy, brother of St. Barnabas and father-in-law of St. Peter; commissioned first bishop of Britain by St. Paul, and consecrated by St. Barnabas, the two apostles to the Gentiles. That Aristobulus was engaged in his mission in Britain when St. Paul wrote his Epistle to the Romans, some years before his first visit, or the visit of any other apostle, to Rome.

12. That Pudens, the husband of Claudia, Claudia herself, her sister Eurgain, her brother Linus, and aunt Pomponia, being converted prior to St. Paul's visit to Rome, the rest of the British royal family, Brân, Caractacus, Cyllinus and Cynon, were converted and baptized by St. Paul himself during his detention in that city preceding his first trial. That the palace of Pudens and Claudia was the home of St. Paul and the other apostles; that their four children, Timotheus, Novatus, Pudentiana and Praxedes, were instructed in the faith by St. Paul; and that Linus, the brother of Claudia and second son of Caractacus, was appointed by the same apostle first bishop of the Church of Rome, such Church meeting at that time, and till the reign of Constantine, in the aforesaid palace, called indifferently "Domus Pudentis, Palatium, Britannicum, Domus Apostolorum, Titulus, Pastor, St. Pudentiana."

13. That after the return of Caractacus to Siluria, St. Paul himself, following the footsteps of his bishop and forerunner, Aristobulus, visited Britain, and confirmed the British Churches in the faith.

14. That the last days of St. Paul, preceding his martyrdom at Rome, were attended by Pudens, Claudia, Linus, Eubulus, whose salutations he sends in his dying charge to Timothy, and that his remains were interred by them in their family sepulchre.

15. That the foundations of the British Church were Apostolical, being coeval, within a few years, with those of the Pentecostal Church at Jerusalem, —preceding those of the primitive Church of Rome,

so far as they were laid by either an apostle or apostolic bishop, by seven years,—preceding the arrival of St. Peter at Rome, as fixed by the great majority of Roman Catholic historians (thirteenth year of Nero), by thirty years,—preceding the first arrival of the papal Church of Rome in Britain, under Augustine, by 456 years.

16. That the British Church has from its origin been a royal one; the royal family of ancient Britain,—of whom our present sovereign is, through the Tudors, the lineal blood representative—being 1. the first British converts to Christianity; 2. the founders of the first Christian institutions in Britain; 3. the chief instruments, in the second century, in the establishment of Christianity as the state religion; and in the fourth century, in the persons of Helen and Constantine the Great, the chief instrument in the aboliton of Paganism, and the substitution, in its place, of Christianity over the whole Roman Empire.

17. That the spiritual or ecclesiastical head of the British Church was always a Briton, resident in Britain, amenable to British laws, and British laws only, and having no superior in the Church but Christ.

18. That whatever may be the religious advantages or disadvantages of the union of the ecclesiastical and civil governments in the person of the Sovereign, such union has been, from the first colonization of our Island, first in Druidic and then in Christian times, the native British, as opposed to the foreign papal—and, in later times, dissenting—principle of their separation.

The Importance to History of the Research by the Rev. Lionel Smithett Lewis, M.A. in 1925

Vicar of Glastonbury, and a wonderful man, Lionel Smithett Lewis shows clearly that the attempt by Dr. Armitage Robinson, Dean of Wells, to rubbish the historic and truthful tradition of St. Joseph of Arimathea, and Glastonbury, was full of hopeless inaccuracy, and a disgrace to the commandment of upholding pure truth.

ST. JOSEPH OF ARIMATHEA,

Died at Glastonbury, a.d. 82.

WHO has not heard that the earliest traditions and the place names of Glastonbury centre round St. Joseph of Arimathea? The tradition of St. Joseph coming and founding the Christian Church here fits in extraordinarily with tradition of other places and with history.

Eusebius (A.D. 260-340), Bishop of Cæsarea, and the Father of Church History after the sacred Canon closed, says : "The Apostles passed beyond the ocean to the isles called the Britannic Isles." Here is very early general corroborative evidence from the Eastern Church of the founding of the British Church in the Apostolic Age. And the primitive silence of the Eastern and Roman Churches as to the post-scripture history of St. Joseph is most significant. His coming to Britain and founding a Church here would account for it. Much of Britain at this time was outside the Roman Empire. For two hundred years from B.C.59, when Julius Cæsar made his first attempt to conquer her, not only was Britain fighting desperately against Rome, but so successfully that during that period every celebrated Roman general fought in Britain. And the Roman Church was too much taken up with her own troubles to think much about what was happening in other contemporary Churches, especially in outlandish parts. This silence about so important a person as St. Joseph is otherwise most strange. The one "honourable councillor" who had the courage to defend Christ in the Council! One of only two men who had the devotion to claim His dead body when all seemed lost ! The story of St. Joseph at Glastonbury seems to explain everything.

GLASTONBURY—

2

Gildas, the British historian (A.D. 516-570), says :
" Meanwhile these islands . . . received the beams of
light, that is, the Holy precepts of Christ, the true Sun
. . . at the latter part, as we know, of the reign of
Tiberius Cæsar."[1] Those words of Gildas, "as we know,"
are peculiarly interesting, being a clear reference to a
generally accepted knowledge, which is striking evidence
from a native son of our native Church, who was its earliest
historian. Nor should we forget that it is claimed that he
lived many years at Glastonbury, and is buried there.[2]
This date, " the latter part of the reign of Tiberius,"
would be at the latest A.D. 37, four years after the
Crucifixion. How well this fits in with the decisions of the
Councils of Pisa, Constance, Sienna, and Basle, that the
British Bishops took precedence of the French and Spanish,
because our Church was founded immediately after the
Passion of Christ !—" Statim post passionem Christi."[3]
An ancient MS., ascribed to Maelgwyn of Llandaff,
said to be the uncle of St. David, which would be about
A.D. 450, tells of St. Joseph's burial in St. Mary's Chapel
(the ancient wattle Church), at Glastonbury, names the site
of his grave (to the south of the altar), and says that he has
with him two vessels, one with the Blood, and the other
with the Sweat of Our Lord.[4]
The celebrated Vatican librarian, Cardinal Baronius,
found an ancient MS. in the Vatican which tells of St.
Joseph, Lazarus, Mary, Martha, and others being put into
an open boat without oars or sails on the Levant, and floating down to, and landing, at Marseilles in A.D. 35.[5] This
fits in with the Marseilles traditions of the settling there of
Lazarus and his sisters, with which that city is saturated.
It must be remembered that histories were few and far
between, and that very many even of these have been
lost. But tradition flourished in the winter nights over the
fireside.
Then there is a tradition in the tin trade that St. Joseph
was a metal merchant.[6] This would mean that he or his
servants must have come to Britain to get tin for bronze.
This, too, would account for his wealth. Tradition says
that he went to Cornwall for tin, and the Somerset hills for

[1] Gildas. Sec. 8.
[2] V. pp. 42-43.
[3] " Disputatio super Dignitatem Angliæ et Galliæ in Concilio
Constantiano." Theodore Martin, Lovar, 1571. These Councils were
held respectively in 1409, 1417, 1424 and 1434.
[4] V. the Author's " St. Joseph of Arimathea at Glastonbury " (3rd
Edn.), p. 25.
[5] V. ditto, p. 24.
[6] V. ditto, p, 17, and v. later pp. 73-75.

other metals.[1] In that case he may have been known as a trader to the celebrated British King Arviragus, and to Glastonbury before he came here as a Missionary.[2]

This brings us to the story of Glastonbury's greatest historian, William of Malmesbury, who was the most critical and accurate of early English historians. He wrote the *"Antiquities of Glastonbury"* about A.D. 1135, at the invitation of the Monks of Glastonbury, after he had written a history of the Kings of the English, and another of the Bishops of the English, some ten years before. There are some obvious additions to his book on Glastonbury as it has reached us. But it is of interest to compare what he wrote about Glastonbury in this book, and what he wrote in the earlier book, the History of the Kings. One sees new phases in his knowledge and his convictions. This critical and truth-loving historian staying at the Abbey, seeing with his eyes the evidence in stone, in processions of pilgrims, and in worship, for men's beliefs, reading the ancient MSS. and books of this once perhaps greatest of British libraries, and drinking in with his ears the traditions of the shrine, and comparing them with the claims of other religious houses, wrote a reasoned and careful history of the place, marking off very clearly certain chapters in its history.

He reminds us that in the persecution, when St. Stephen was slain, all the disciples except the apostles were scattered from Jerusalem. This fits in with the date of St. Joseph and the family at Bethany being placed in the boat. And who more likely to awaken the animosity of the Jews? William quotes Freculphus, Bishop of Lisieux in the ninth century, as having recorded that St. Philip the Apostle went to France to preach. He then adds that St. Philip sent twelve men from France (to which the Vatican MS. traced St. Joseph), to convert Britain, of whom St. Joseph of Arimathea, St. Philip's " dearest friend," was leader. He gives the date as A.D. 63. The different date need not upset us. We must expect differences of detail in these ancient stories.

[1] There must be something distinctive about Mendip or British metal. At Ostia, the sea-port of Rome, there was found not long ago an ancient Roman drain-pipe below the chariot-road. It was a particularly good specimen and was bonded in some special way with tin. Professor Russell Forbes cut off a section and sent it home to England without comment for analysis. The verdict was that the metal came from Mendip mines.

[2] Diodorus Siculus, writing just before Christ, traces the route of the tin merchants from Marseilles to Cornwall. There is a traditional route from the tin mines of Cornwall to the lead mines of the Mendips in Somerset, some traces of which perhaps exist. V. Taylor's " The Coming of the Saints," pp. 178-180.

He records that the great King Arviragus remained
unconverted, but that he was kind to the missionaries and
that three kings, Arviragus, and afterwards his son Marius,
and later Coel (who is buried at Glastonbury), Marius'
successor, between them granted them twelve hides of
land.[1] It was probably as a sign that Arviragus had given
the land that St. Joseph planted his staff, which tradition
says grew into the Holy Thorn, an object of pilgrimage and
veneration all down the middle ages. Arviragus' grant was
the beginning of the famous " Twelve Hides of Glaston,"
which is the name of a territorial hundred to this day. The
Twelve Hides enormously expanded beyond twelve actual
hides. It is worth noting that 1,000 years later, in that
great tax-book, Domesday Book, it is recorded that these
twelve hides had never paid tax. Part of the hides given
by Arviragus himself was " Ynnis Witrin," an ancient
Celtic name for Glastonbury meaning probably the Crystal
Isle, "an island surrounded by thickets, woods and
marshes." William tells us that they were warned by St.
Gabriel to build a church in honour of the Blessed Virgin
Mary, which they did of twisted twigs. This is the
celebrated Wattle Church, " The Ecclesia Vetusta," " The
Olde Church," St. Joseph's Chapel, probably the first
above-ground Church in the world, the Mother Church of
Britain. All down the ages it has been esteemed the most
sacred spot in Britain. William cites " written evidence
of good credit found at St. Edmund's to this effect : The
Church of Glastonbury did none other men's hands make,
but actual disciples of Christ built it, being sent by St.
Philip the Apostle, as was said before." [2] He further tells
us : " Thereupon the twelve Saints—so often mentioned—
paying devout homage in that same spot to God and the
Blessed Virgin, spending the time in vigils, fasts, and
prayers, were constantly sustained . . . The said
Saints continued to live in the same hermitage for many
years, and were at last liberated from the prison of the
flesh. The place then began to be a covert for wild beasts
—the spot which had before been the habitation of Saints—
until the Blessed Virgin was pleased to recall her House
of Prayer to the memory of the faithful." [3]

All the geography and folk lore of Glastonbury speak
of St. Joseph. To the south-west of the town stands
Weary-all Hill, the ancient Wirral, the hill where he and

---

[1] William of Malmesbury's De Antiquitate, Cap. 1 and 33. Lomax'
translation is used throughout.
[2] De Antiquitate, Cap. 2.
[3] De Antiquitate, Cap. 1.

his companions are said to have landed.   The name was too
tempting not to be converted in the course of ages to
Weary-all, to denote the condition of the tired travellers.
The sea came up to it in those days.   What are now some
seventeen miles of marshes were then awash.   As recently
as Stuart days a tidal wave reached St. Benignus' Church
in the lower part of the town.   Standing on the Tor Hill
on a moonlight night, with the valley bathed in mists, you
can get a very clear and beautiful picture of how the island
stood out of the water in those distant days.   And a less
beautiful scene in the daylight when the floods are out also
helps one to understand.   But it does not absolutely trans-
late one as the moon and the mist do with only the help of
a very little imagination.   Then one might be living at the
moment.   And the sight of St. Joseph with his staff and
his companions would seem fitting.   That staff that became
the world-famed Holy Thorn that blossoms at Christmas !
Although the original tree was destroyed by a fanatical
Puritan, who paid the penalty of his deed,[1] and although the
shoots cannot be struck, ere the venerable tree followed its
persecutor to the grave, loving hands budded and grafted
it, and its descendants are with us to-day, a Levantine
Thorn, hailing from the same land as St. Joseph, which
has never ceased to flower at Christmas, and gives us its
sweet flowers in the spring as well.   Practically never without leaf, from October till May with buds on its boughs, it
bears an immemorial ever-present testimony to the story
of St. Joseph.   The site of the present Vicarage was
chosen because the oldest and finest existing specimen of
the Holy Thorn of Glaston stood in what was enclosed as
its garden.   There are less good trees in the Abbey ground,
and in the Churchyard.   And even in America and the
Colonies they are growing.   Then at the foot of the Tor,
that tower-crowned hill which dominates Somerset, and
can be seen from the borders of Devon and Gloucestershire,
is another almost eternal thing that speaks of St. Joseph—
the Chalice Well.   Its name commemorates what he
brought from the Holy Land.   More than 2,000 years ago
it was a sacred well of the Druids, before it became a sacred
Christian well, before the worship of the Sun had ceased on
the commanding hill, and a Church of the Crucified (alas,
now in ruins), proclaimed Christ from its summit.   Pure
and limpid it pours its waters forth.   Within the memory
of man they have never failed.   They are as sure as the
secret of its source is uncertain.   That secret it has kept

[1] V. the Author's " St. Joseph of Arimathea at Glastonbury " (3rd
Edn.), pp. 11-12.

all down the ages. But when all the skill of modern science fails, without a change of countenance it simply and naturally steps in and supplies man's need, rivers of living water that never fail, a type of what St. Joseph brought, when he and his companions came and lived within its spell.[1]

Cressy, the Benedictine Monk and Historian, who was versed in the traditions of the great Benedictine Monastery of Glastonbury, which were treasured among the Continental Benedictine houses, tells us that St. Joseph of Arimathea died at Glastonbury on July 27th, A.D. 82. Once he had hewn out of the living rock at some cost a far away tomb for himself. But the Christ came into his life, and that tomb. And the "honourable councillor," the rich man, rose from his dead self, and died a russet-clad hermit, and was buried in a wicker Church in far-off Britain.

ST. ARISTOBULUS.[2]

BURIED AT GLASTONBURY A.D. 99.

The name of Aristobulus, the companion and fellow-worker of St. Paul, is associated with Glastonbury. Though, alas, owing to the flood of heathendom which temporarily swamped the greater part of this country after the first few centuries, the fact has been too much forgotten by our Church, there is steady testimony from the Eastern Church that St. Aristobulus was the first Bishop of the Britons. St. Dorotheus, Bishop of Tyre, A.D. 303, wrote : "Aristobulus, whom Paul saluted, writing to the Romans, was Bishop of Britain."[3] Haleca, Bishop of Augusta, said, "The memory of many martyrs is celebrated by the Britons, especially that of St. Aristobulus, one of the seventy disciples."[4] And the same fact is more fully recorded in the Martyrologies of the Greek Church. The Greek Menology for 15th March reads thus : "Aristobulus was one of the seventy disciples, and a follower of St. Paul the Apostle, along with whom he preached the Gospel to the whole world, and ministered to him. He was chosen by St. Paul to be the missionary bishop to the land of Britain, *inhabited by a very warlike and fierce race. By them he* was often scourged, and repeatedly dragged as a criminal

[1] Unfailingly it yields 20,000 gallons a day, Miss A. M. Buckton, its owner, says.
[2] V. the Author's " St. Joseph of Arimathea at Glastonbury " (3rd Edn.), pp. 7, 10, 28-30 and 32.
[3] Synopsis de Apostol : Synops 23 " Aristobulus."
[4] Halecae Fragmenta in Martyr.

were his empty shield and his full shield ever before them
on the great Pilgrims' Inn, and they knew what it all meant.
His full shield was on the chest protecting their Church
accounts, and the deeds of their property in the Church.
His story on the alms-basin did not inspire them as their
alms were offered, because alms were not offered in that
way in their day. But they gave their alms all the same,
and for St. George. The dry old Church accounts give
us peeps into the every-day life as well as the strictly
Church life of that day. And we learn that on St. George's
Day players came, and larger sums were reaped from the
play than on any other day. And poor old people had
alms distributed among them. In 1418 they restored their
Chapel of St. George, and the Suffragan Bishop came and
consecrated a new Altar there. There was a painted
banner of St. George in it. There was a relic of St. George
kept under lock and key. And there was an image of
George evidently on horseback set on high, but like everything else, it grew old. For in 1500 the horse required a new
tail, and one John Chyverton, a painter, re-gilded the
image, which must have been a large one, for he got paid
very highly for doing it, receiving no less than £6 13s. 4d.,
equal to about £60 in these days, if not more. Evidently
women and girls were taught especially to venerate St.
George, the deliverer of Princess Sabra, for the girls of the
Church subscribed £1 13s. 4d. towards this work, and the
women 13s. 4d., more than one-third of the whole cost.

No, no, no, if St. George belong to England—and what
Englishman would allow a foreigner to say that he did not?
—"St. George for England!" England owes him to
Coventry and Glastonbury. Coventry gave him birth:
Glastonbury armed him, and taught him to be a great and
good knight. Then the English wanderlust came on him
and, being what we made him, the rest of the world heard
of him.

THE MOST WONDERFUL TRADITION OF ALL.

CHRIST AT GLASTONBURY.

Did Our Lord ever come to Glastonbury as a lad?
The story not only lingers here, but elsewhere. Briefly,
the tradition is this : That Our Lord accompanied St. Joseph
of Arimathea as a lad on one of the Saint's expeditions to
Britain to seek metal. For the possibilities of this legend,

and for the other legends and facts that fit in with it, I must quote my "*St. Joseph of Arimathea at Glastonbury*" (Third Edition, pp.17-18) :

"Perhaps there is some truth in the strange tradition which still lingers, not only among the hill folk of Somerset, but of Gloucestershire,[1] that St. Joseph of Arimathea came to Britain first as a metal merchant seeking tin from the Scillys and Cornwall, and lead, copper and other metals from the hills of Somerset, and that Our Lord Himself came with him as a boy. There is also a tradition in the West of Ireland that Our Lord came to Glastonbury as a boy.[2] The tradition is so startling that the first impulse is summarily to reject it as ridiculous. But certain it is that it is most persistent. And certain it is that amongst the old tin-workers, who have always observed a certain mystery in their rites, there was a moment when they ceased their work, and started singing a quaint song beginning ' Joseph was in the tin trade.' Mr. Henry Jenner, F.S.A., late of the British Museum, narrates that some years back in North London during the making of tin sheets for organ pipes, before the molten metal was poured,[4] a man said every time, ' Joseph was in the tin trade.' And certain it is that if St. Joseph was a metal merchant he must somehow have got tin for bronze, and that Britain is almost the sole land for tin mines. And if he were a metal merchant, it is not inconsistent with his being a rich man. And the strange story of Our Lord's coming which is so very dear to simple Somerset hearts would be explained by the Eastern tradition that St. Joseph was the uncle of the Blessed Virgin Mary.[5] So if there be any truth in the ancient story, this old hill—" The Tor "—with its rites may have attracted the mart which first led here St. Joseph and the Redeemer before He began His ministry. And to it, after the wondrous Resurrection and Ascension, St. Joseph, laden with the New Message of the New Religion would wend his way on his mission from Gaul to Britain, the seat of Druidism. His knowledge of the Druids would account (in part) for his kindly reception by the Druids of France,

[1] The Ven. Walter Farrer, Archdeacon of Wells, told me that the legend is to be met with in Gloucestershire.
[2] The Rev. Canon A. R. B. Young, Prebendary of Clogher Cathedral in Ireland, has heard the tradition all his life.
[3] V. also Baring Gould's " Cornwall," p. 57.
[4] Quarterly Review of the Benedictines of Caldey, 1916, pp. 135-6.
[5] It is curious that King Arthur claimed descent from St. Joseph, and St. David, said to be his uncle, was said to be of kin to the Blessed Virgin Mary. For the descent of King Arthur from St. Joseph, see John of Glastonbury (Hearne's Edition), Vol. I., pp. 56-57 (small paper), where it is set out. He was 8th in descent.

and he would come to King Arviragus, or at any rate some
of his subjects, as a not unknown person, and hence,
perhaps, his kindly reception and the donation of land."
    There is a tradition, too, at Marazion, in Cornwall, of
St. Joseph coming there to trade with tin miners. Mara-
zion means " bitter Zion." Its other name is still Market
Jew. And it is a most ancient tradition that it was a colony
of Jews who traded in tin. " Jews' houses," " Jews' tin,"
" Jews' leavings," " Jews' pieces," are still common terms
in the Cornish tin mines. The oldest pits containing smelted
tin are called " Jews' houses." [1]
    William Blake, the poet (1757-1827), had evidently
heard the tradition of Glastonbury, and embalmed it in
beautiful verses, to which Hubert Parry wedded equally
inspired music. With these I will end :—

JERUSALEM.

" And did those feet in ancient time
    " Walk upon England's mountains green ?
" And was the Holy Lamb of God
    " In England's pleasant pastures seen ?
" And did the Countenance Divine
    " Shine forth upon our clouded hills ?
" And was Jerusalem builded here
    " Among those dark Satanic mills ?

" Bring me my bow of burning gold !
    " Bring me my arrows of desire !
" Bring me my spear ! O clouds, unfold !
    " Bring me my Chariot of Fire !
" I will not cease from mental fight ;
    " Nor shall my sword sleep in my hand
" Till I have built Jerusalem
    " In England's green and pleasant land."

[1] V. Taylor's " Coming of the Saints," pp. 182-3. And v. also
pp. 178-180 for the route of the tin merchants from Marseilles to
Cornwall before Christ.

SCRYING IN THE MANNER OF THE HIGH PRIESTS IN THE TEMPLE OF SOLOMON USING URIM & THUMMIN

The Effects of Scrying

Scrying Using Crystals

In my last book, The Voyages of Joseph of Avalon, my scrying was in the manner of the Druids using a Crystal Skull, Crystal Ball, and Crystal Wand, using trance meditation. The experiment was good fun, I walked around the garden offering each crystal in turn; skull, wand and crystal ball, to the North, South, East and West; returning to my seat in the centre of a circle facing the setting sun. I enjoyed the experience. With a health warning in the book, that the results should be regarded as entertainment only.

Scrying Using the Urim & Thummin

Scrying in the manner of the High Priests in the Temple of Solomon, in Jerusalem, using the Urim & Thummin comprising of twelve precious and semiprecious stones, set into a breast plate, with the aid of Wilson the skeleton. The experiment was not a pleasant experience, because the after effects from coming out from the trance meditation. These lasted for around a week, it is an experiment in parapsychology I am not likely to repeat. Using trance meditation, I chose to use Wilson in order to place myself in the extended chain in order not to offend Jewish people, by taking on the role of a Jewish High Priest, a position for which I do not qualify.

Wilson the Skeleton
wearing the Urim and Thummin

AN EXPERIMENT IN
PARAPSYCHOLOGY

These experiments, Scrying in the manner of the High Priests at the temple of Solomon in Jerusalem, using the Urim and Thummin, must be regarded as for entertainment only, and having no basis in fact. This section is not for those of a nervous disposition or the faint hearted.

SCRYING IN THE MANNER OF
THE HIGH PRIESTS IN THE
TEMPLE OF SOLOMON

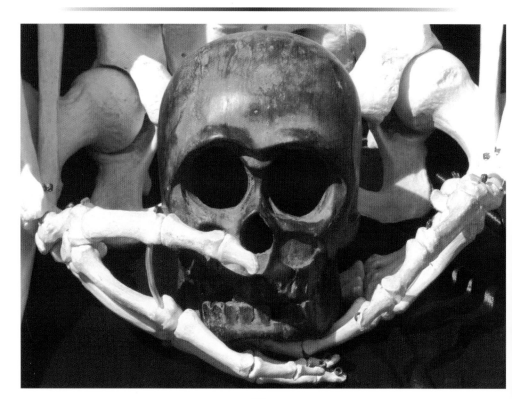

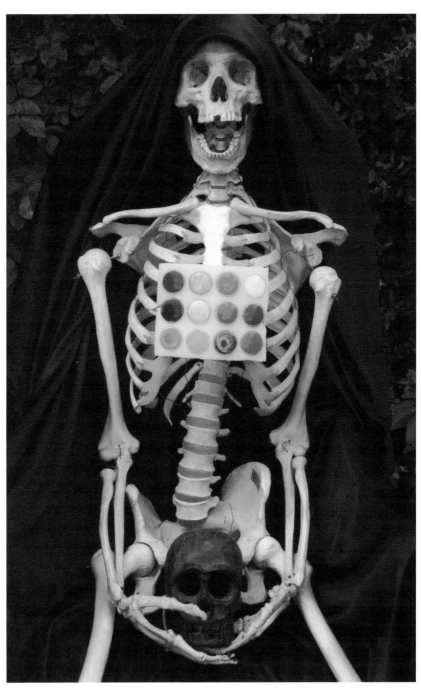

Wilson the skeleton holding the **SKULL** OF **DOOM**

THE SKULL OF DOOM

I sat in my chair in my garden, with the sun going down preparing to enter trance meditation holding the hand of Wilson the skeleton sitting next to me.

In my pocket was my piece of Calvary given to me by Sister Katerina who tended the Altar of Crucifixion in the Holy Sepulchre when I was filming my Documentary Jerusalem. I always held the piece of Calvary in my hand during my prayer for protection before scrying. Whilst I felt confident scrying with the Skull of Doom, I did not feel inclined to hold the skull during the proceedings. I decided to leave that pleasure to Wilson the skeleton who was wearing the Urim and Thummin, as worn by the High Priests when scrying in the Temple of Solomon. Inside the small pots on Wilsons Breastplate were real precious and semi precious stones, as used at the time. Wilson sat with us at the dining table during our afternoon strawberry tea, to set the mood of preparation.

What I saw during the scrying was in vivid technicolour and quite scary.

SCRYING WITH: THE SKULL OF DOOM

I Saw a Great Skeleton, Striding the Oceans, Calling to Me. My Waters are Warming My Prophet.

My Fish and My Creatures will Die. Great will be My Wrath, Upon Those who have Poisoned My Soul. I will Sack My Land. I will Return It to the Sea. I will Burn the Land. I will Burn the Forests. I will Flood the Coasts and Cities, until I have Washed Away the Poison. Poison will Rise from the Depths of My Oceans. There will be Wars with those Who Try to Escape My Wrath .Man will Destroy Himself and his Filthy Ways. Keep Watch on the Night of the High Tides. Do Not Sleep, Less you Perish in My Waters. Keep Watch when My Sun is Hot, Less you Perish in the Heat.

My Punishments are Coming. I will Passover Those I Love, and Those Who Love Me, and Keep My Commandments, or Repent Their Evil Ways, I will Not Take Away Their Time and Eternity. Others Who are Not of My Way, Shall Perish in My Waters, the Poisoned Air, or Burnt by My Sun.

My Earth Shall Not be, Entirely Destroyed by My Waters.

A Stone, Uncut by Human Hand, Shall Fall from the Heavens. A Great Mountain will Arise Upon the Earth. My Divine Punishment will Cease. A New Age will Begin.

SCRYING IN THE MANNER OF THE HIGH PRIESTS IN THE TEMPLE OF SOLOMON

SCRYING WITH THE CRYSTAL SKULL

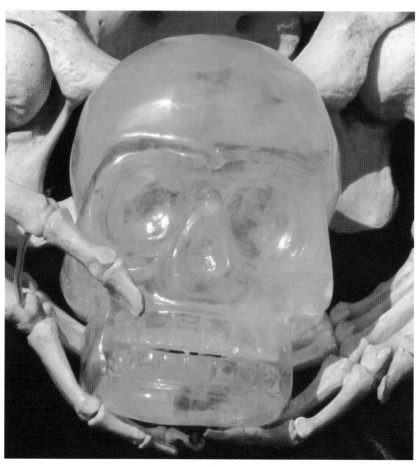

THE CRYSTAL SKULL

I found myself looking down on the planet as if in a space station. I had the sense that the damaging effects of excessive heat, the warming of the oceans through ice loss, and more frequent storms and torrential downpours, that will bring widespread flooding and flooding of rivers, is way ahead of the catastrophe resulting from expansion of water in the oceans and the coming rise in sea levels.

BRITAIN

Looking down on Britain at the counties below the Rayner line, discussed in my previous book, a line running from the Isle of Wight off the South coast of England to the Wash, in the Midlands. The East Coast was becoming like the South of France in temperatures and weather patterns. That is the South of France as it used to be before it was burnt out by the sun.

Above the line towards the West of England and Wales, continuous downpours lasting five days were washing away crops, drowning farm animals and causing rivers to rise and merge into great floods. The equivalent of four weeks rainfall was falling in a single day. The flooding was washing out power stations, reservoirs and water purification plants, and factories. A new triangular lake appeared from Worcester to Stow on the Wold and Leamington Spa.

Looking round the coast, there was no discernable rise in sea levels. Although severe storms at sea, mainly from the west, battered coastlines. Hurricanes from the North Atlantic were hitting Ireland, Wales and Scotland. Areas of coastlines in North East England were being eroded into the North Sea.

In Scotland, short 2/3 week winter events of arctic conditions brought Aberdeen and Edinburgh to a standstill.

SPAIN

Looking over to Spain, temperatures had climbed to 48°. Water was in short supply, and fires raged everywhere. People were heading to airports in their thousands, flying to Britain and elsewhere in Europe. Others were delayed on roads due to fires.

ITALY

Temperatures were reaching 50° destroying crops, plant growth and causing fires. Even Northern Italy suffered serious effects of high temperatures. Parts of Southern Italy were becoming uninhabitable due to fires and shortage of water. The level of the water in the river system through Germany, Italy and France dropped dramatically.

FRANCE

Northern France was hot, such that in some towns, including Paris a heat haze was rising from roof tops. It appeared that the elderly were being ferried to hospitals.

Southern France appeared to be seriously affected across to Italy. Fires raged everywhere. Crops and vineyards were ablaze. People were leaving on a massive scale as water with which to tackle fires ran out.

TURKEY

Temperatures in Turkey were excessively high, but what caught my attention was an earthquake across the Sea of Marmara to Istanbul. Followed almost instantaneously by earthquakes in Italy and Greece. I can best describe the events as an instantaneous cluster of earthquakes, not an earthquake event to which we have become accustomed, or have seen in the past, to the best of my knowledge. Much of Greece was on fire.

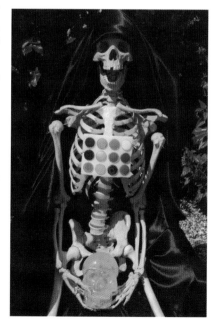

RUSSIA

Most of the former Soviet Union was largly unaffected by global warming. Many areas came into use for farming.

SCRYING IN THE MANNER OF THE HIGH PRIESTS IN THE TEMPLE OF SOLOMON

SCRYING WITH THE ARMAGEDDON SKULL

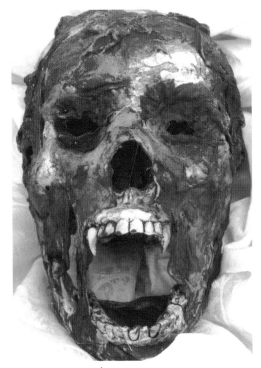

AMERICA

L ooking down on America, there was wide spread suffering I did not want to see, because we all love our American cousins.

Global warming was causing major unexpected weather events across many states. A change in the weather pattern in the Pacific brought a grim drought to America's Southwest. Greater warming of land mass and drought was drying up the Colorado River basin affecting the availability of drinking water of millions of Americans. South West America was becoming desert. The Colerado river became eventually nothing more than a trickle. Crops were failing in a big way over huge areas of farm land. Soil was turning to dust. Winds caused black blizzards across a million acres from Texas to Dakota. There appeared to be no end in sight for the misery that followed a line from Colorado to Las Vegas across to Phoenix. There was mass movement of people to North America and Canada to water. The East coast of America told a very different story. The North Atlantic was very wet indeed. Water vapour held in the clouds was changing the sea temperatures in the North Atlantic.

Looking up towards the Arctic there was no sea ice to speak of, but there did not appear to be any significant rise in sea levels. There was undersea volcanic activity in the mid atlantic causing tsunamis. Looking in the opposite direction storms are constantly battering into the Gulf of Mexico turning into hurricanes of significant strength. However one of the storms or hurricanes had missed the gulf and was heading up towards Washington and New York gaining strength all the while. This storm event caused sea water to flood into subways causing chaos. There was no area along the coast that was not affected by this stray storm. Finally I saw what looked like a tsunami out to sea along a line from San Francisco to Vancouver in Canada.

CENTRAL AFRICA

Looking across the South Atlantic to Central Africa, the land was parched; fires raged everywhere. Dead cattle, skeletons, and dead people were all around. There was a dark shadow which in parapsychological terms implies an extinction. I do not choose to elaborate further.

ASIA

Turning to Asia, war was raging everywhere. Bangladesh had become part of the sea. Millions were battling to get into India and China. Troops and aircraft were using all manner of weapons to keep them out. I looked away. Would it were that I had not seen such misery in Bangladesh, India and Pakistan where violent monsoon rain brought devastating floods and human misery.

AUSTRALIA

Apart from small areas in the North and West, Australia became a desert.

HAVING SEEN THE COMING EFFECTS FROM GLOBAL WARMING, NO ONE SHOULD BLAME GOD

STOP BLAMING GOD

In the late 1960's, I spent six months working with a wonderfully talented and great man in every respect, whose job it was to produce and direct mounted outside broadcast programmes for the Sunday Services on T.V.

Having trained and worked in almost every job in a television studio and outside broadcast unit, there was not much I did not know about making a television programme. What the job did afford me was the opportunity to enjoy long discussions with some quite senior clergy in both the Catholic Church and Church of England, during the drives to the various venues.

One question that always came under discussion, and continues to arise on both T.V. and radio even 45 years later is this; "how do I explain to my flock why God did not prevent this flood, or that storm, or the disaster that has ruined livelihoods and lives in my Diocese?"

The answer was and remains simple. Tell your congregation to stop blaming God. God has nothing to do with these disasters.

Planet Earth is a living, independent entity. It has a tectonic plate system that by subduction, moves great continents under each other about one millimeter per year. This live, moving system alone is responsible for volcanic eruptions, earthquakes and tsunamis. Planet Earth also has a giant weather system that ranges across the whole plant. The temperatures of Earth's oceans affect weather patterns around the globe. Then there are the ice ages followed by the melting of the ice ages, fetching the coming of the very warm periods in Earth's history.

All these systems are connected in ways that are not yet fully understood by scientists. All these systems march onwards every minute of every day doing their own thing. The Earth and its complex Earth systems have their own existence completely independent of man.

If man chooses to live on a fault line within an Earth quake zone, or a flood plain, or near rivers that flood, or close to the shore line in and around Indonesia, where catastrophic events will happen. What has that to do with God?

Almighty God does not cause or bring about these disasters; they happen because that is how our planet works.
Man pays little or no regard to living in dangerous areas, and to prove the point, when there is an earthquake, flood or any other Earth made disaster, man will be quick to rebuild his residence and life on the same spot that the disaster took place. Man will even build suburbia where disaster has taken place.

God, or The Powers of The Universe exist completely outside the physical structure of this planet. So please stop making excuses for, or blaming God for every disaster. God has absolutely nothing to do with them.

Yes, we can still pray to God for a miracle, but such prayers would be for a miracle of healing for example, and this miracle can happen. However, this is a completely different topic for a different book.

GLASTONBURY
SAINTS

by

Sylvia Rayner

AVALON, THE ROYAL ISLE, THE HOLY ISLE
THE ISLE OF DEPARTED SPIRITS
THE ISLE OF THE IMMORTALS
THE GLASS ISLAND

The Saints of Glastonbury, so many, so special, gathering here for safety. They all play their part on Englands pleasant pastures.

The magic of the place drew them all to the home of Jesus and Joseph of Avalon. They made the history of Britain, kept alive by their works and writings of the Monks. King Arthur, King Ina, both Saints for their works and suffering for the Christian faith. At some time in their lives the Saints of the world have had connections with Glastonbury. The most holy place in Britain, from the Beginning.

IN A HEART BEAT

Yes, I can hear you Saints of the Past
Gathering here in every corner
Until I cry and shudder at the thought of your suffering.

I will try not to run from my dreams.
Memories of the time we spent together
Building this glorious Abbey on the secret Isle of Avalon.

I hear the whisperings that come and go
On the morning breeze Eerie they call it.

What great future have you to tell?
The answer comes to me in dreams I am baffled!
I saw you there but you Vanished and left me with a hundred questions.

Arthur turned and smiled at me My heart gave way
And I knew Glastonbury was to be loved
And the Saints cherished with every breath.

Our dreams we cannot stop the Past is the Present
So may this be with Avalon.

Sylvia Rayner

One of the Most Famous Saints
of Glastonbury

St. Dunston the Bell Maker
The Patron Saint of Goldsmiths

Born on Candlemas Day, of Parents Quendied and Herston within the twelve hides of Glastonbury.

Dunston was a gifted craftsman. A competent goldsmith making chalices and goblets. He worked with metals as bell maker and clock maker. This tradition continued well into the 14th Century when bells and clocks for Wells, Exeter Cathedral and Wimborne Minster continued to be made at Glastonbury by Peter Lightfoot. Dunston's forge and workshop was where he lived, worked and prayed, keeping busy and loving every moment.

St. Dunston schooled at the Abbey, and as we know, later became the Abbot, the equivalent to a Prime Minister today.

His birthday has been recorded as 925 AD but research shows more probably 909 AD. Yes, he was well taught, an advantage when you descend from Royal Blood.

In the Courts of King Athelston, he mixed with Archbishops and Kings, aware of politics and foreign trade. Encouraged by the King who respected his knowledge, he soon emerged as a Monk.

Abbots of the Royal Isle of Glastonbury in the days of Celts, Saxons and Normans came from Royal descent. Their children, the Sons of Kings were sent to the Druid Cor, and taught for the fifteen years as tradition following the footsteps of Jesus and Adnam. St. Dunston was made Abbott when he was just 31 years old, and later as we know The twenty-third Archbishop of Canterbury.

Tradition has it that he was buried at Canterbury, but other scholars prefer his remains to be in his beloved Glastonbury Abbey.
This is no problem, and Dunston would be quite amused to think that in the 21 Century, someone cares!

Called the 'Honourable Councillor' because of his support he gave to Jesus, and how he managed to take Jesus down from the cross with the help of Nicademus, before the Romans broke the legs of Jesus and, as was their practice in those days, drag the victim through the streets. The family did not have to witness this, but brought the soothing oils and spices to sooth the body of Jesus. The spices gathered from other lands. Spices and herbs used by the Druids for healing and arranged by Joseph of Avalon for the ritual cherished upon your loved one.

The only known carving of Joseph of Arimathea

Note: Joseph of Arimathea died AD 81 and was buried at Glastonbury

THE KING OF AVALON

Thousands gathered at the Glass lake
To say goodbye to their dear Joseph.
Kings stood in honour in an all night vigil, fires still glowing.
Flames from the lamps creating a solemn scene.

No man can imagine the splendour.
Druids in their purple robes each wearing the Urim and Thummin,
Sparkling with the jewels in the light of dawn.
Precious stones, gifts from Joseph.

By now the mist was passing revealing the tiny crafts,
Covered in the small dark people of the lake.
The dark mystics wearing the black.
Lamps glinting like the fairy folk themselves.
They were silent, carrying the sprigs of the Holy Thorn,
As tribute to Joseph, their King.

The chanting and singing became as one,
All celebrating the life of this unique man who knew and loved Jesus.
Sweet Joseph dear friend you must go.
Continue your journey.
Do not fear, we hold your love here
In our hearts.

Joseph closed his eyes and remembered dear Jesus
who guided him and set him on the path of life.
His first voyage with Jesus, and his last.
The first Church at Avalon.
And the sweetness of the place.

Time to leave.
Do not be sad for I am with Jesus.
I see his face
I see his smile
I am in heaven

Sylvia Rayner

BURIED AT GLASTONBURY
ST. ARISTOBULUS
DIED IN AD 99.

The brother of St. Barnabas, he became the first Bishop of Britain and companion of St. Paul. St. Barnabas became one of the 70 disciples to follow St. Paul preaching the gospel to the whole world.

KING INA
668 - 725 AD

King Ina of Wessex who loved Glastonbury with great passion, as many do today.

Before the Great Church of Glastonbury was built, our King Ina with all his love built a 'really great church' on to Joseph's humble dwelling, gave grants of his lands and gifts. Then said goodbye and taking his Queen Ethelburga departed to Rome, where he spent his time in humble dwelling.

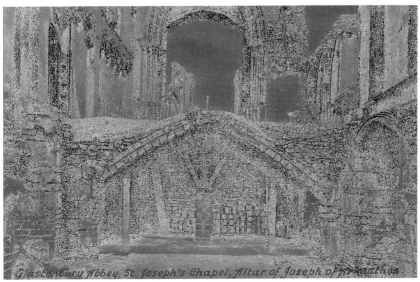

Postcard Dated 1905
Glastonbury Abbey, ST. JOSEPH'S CHAPEL, Altar of Joseph of Arimathea

KING ARTHUR

On the death of his father Arthur was crowned by Dubricus Archbishop of Caerleon. Arthur was just 15 years old.

He loved his sword, his famous sword which was called Calliburn forged in Avalon. Secretly inside his shield a beautiful painting of 'the Blessed Virgin and child', this is carried to all his battles.

After the Wars a great assembly was gathered at Caerleon on Usk. It was the feast of Pentecost all Kings of the Kingdom, together with three Archbishops from Caerleon, York and London.

This was a great assembly, never to be forgotten, when Arthur was crowned once again by Dubricus at a time of peace in the Country.

WILLIAM OF MALMESBURY

William of Malmesbury writes in his book with wonderful reference to chalices, Lancelot Of the Lake, King Arthur and the Holy Grail. 'The Book of the Acts of the illustrious King Arthur'.

He tells of a furious battle fought with Modred near the River Camba, where both armies were killed. Arthur was badly wounded and carried to the Isle of Avalon, beloved Glastonbury, where he gave his crown to Constantine the son of Cador, Duke of Cornwall. This took place in 542 AD

He tells of how 'Arthur the Illustrious' was buried in the Monks Cemetery between two pyramidal stones along with his spouse. This being the last place anyone would think of looking.

THE PASSING OF ARTHUR

So all day long the noise of battle roll'd
Among the mountains by the winter sea ;
Until King Arthur's Table, man by man,
Had fall'n in Lyonesse about their lord,
King Arthur. Then, because his wound was deep,
The bold Sir Bedivere uplifted him,
And bore him to a chapel nigh the field,

A broken chancel with a broken cross,
That stood on a dark strait of barren land :
On one side lay the Ocean and on one
Lay a great water, and the moon was full.
Then spoke King Arthur to Sir Bedivere :
" The sequel of to-day unsoldiers all
The goodliest fellowship of famous Knights
Whereof this world holds record. Such a sleep
They sleep—the men I loved. I think that we
Shall never more, at any future time,
Delight our souls with talk of knightly deeds,
Walking about the gardens and the halls
Of Camelot, as in the days that were.
I perish by this people which I made,—
Tho' Merlin sware that I should come again
To rule once more ; but let what will be, be.
I am so deeply smitten thro' the helm
That without help I cannot last till morn.
Thou therefore take my brand Excalibur,
Which was my pride ; for thou rememberest how
In those old days, one summer noon, an arm
Rose up from out the bosom of the lake,
Clothed in white samite, mystic, wonderful,
Holding the sword—and how I rowed across
And took it, and have worn it, like a king ;
And, wheresoever I am sung or told
In aftertime, this also shall be known ;
But now delay not ; take Excalibur,
And fling him far into the middle mere :
Watch what thou seëst, and lightly bring me word."

Then quickly rose Sir Bedivere, and ran,
And, leaping down the ridges lightly, plunged
Among the bulrush-beds, and clutch'd the sword,
And strongly wheel'd and threw it. The great brand
Made lightnings in the splendour of the moon,
And flashing round and round, and whirl'd in an arch,
Shot like a streamer of the northern morn,
Seen where the moving isles of winter shock
By night, with noises of the northern sea.
So flash'd and fell the brand Excalibur :

But ere he dipt the surface, rose an arm
Clothed in white samite, mystic, wonderful,
And caught him by the hilt, and brandish'd him
Three times, and drew him under in the mere,
And lightly went the other to the king.
Then spoke King Arthur, drawing thicker breath :
" Now see I by thine eyes that this is done.
Speak out : What is it thou hast heard, or seen ? "
And answer made the bold Sir Bedivere :
" Sir King, I closed mine eyelids, lest the gems
Should blind my purpose, for I never saw,
Nor shall see, here or elsewhere, till I die,
Not tho' I live three lives of mortal men,
So great a miracle as yonder hilt,
Then with both hands I flung him, wheeling him ;
But when I look'd again, behold an arm,
Clothed in white samite, mystic, wonderful,
That caught him by the hilt, and brandish'd him
Three times, and drew him under in the mere."
And answer made King Arthur, breathing hard :
" My end draws nigh ; 'tis time that I were gone.
Make broad thy shoulders to receive my weight,
And bear me to the margin ; yet I fear
My wound hath taken cold, and I shall die."
So saying, from the pavement he half rose,
Slowly, with pain, reclining on his arm,
And looking wistfully with wide blue eyes
As in a picture.   Him Sir Bedivere
Remorsefully regarded thro' his tears,
And would have spoken, but he found not words ;
Then took with care, and kneeling on one knee,
O'er both his shoulders drew the languid hands,
And rising bore him thro' the place of tombs.
But, as he walk'd King Arthur panted hard,
Like one that feels a nightmare on his bed
When all the house is mute.   So sigh'd the King,
Muttering and murmuring at his ear " Quick, quick !
I fear it is too late, and I shall die."
But the other swiftly strode from ridge to ridge,
Clothed with his breath, and looking, as he walk'd,

Larger than human on the frozen hills.
He heard the deep behind him, and a cry
Before.   His own thought drove him like a goad,
Dry clash'd his harness in the icy caves
And barren chasms, and all to left and right
The bare black cliff clang'd round him, as he based
His feet on juts of slippery crag that rang
Sharp-smitten with the dint of armed heels—
And on a sudden, lo ! the level lake,
And the long glories of the winter moon.
Then saw they how there hove a dusky barge,
Dark as a funeral scarf from stem to stern,
Beneath them ; and descending they were ware
That all the decks were dense with stately forms,
Black-stoled, black-hooded, like a dream—by these
Three Queens with crowns of gold : and from them rose
A cry that shiver'd to the tingling stars,
And, as it were one voice, an agony
Of lamentation, like a wind that shrills
All night in a waste land, where no one comes,
Or hath come, since the making of the world.
Then murmur'd Arthur, " Place me in the barge " ;
So to the barge they came.   There those three
Put forth their hands, and took the King, and wept.
But she, that rose the tallest of them all
And fairest, laid his head upon her lap,
And loosed the shatter'd casque, and chafed his hands,
And call'd him by his name, complaining loud,
And dropping bitter tears against his brow
Striped with dark blood : for all his face was white
And colourless, and like the wither'd moon
Smote by the fresh beam of the springing east ;
And all his greaves and cuisses dash'd with drops
Of onset ; and the light and lustrous curls—
That made his forehead like a rising sun
High from the daïs-throne—were parch'd with dust ;
Or, clotted into points and hanging loose,
Mix'd with the knightly growth that fringed his lips.
So like a shatter'd column lay the King ;
Not like that Arthur who, with lance in rest,

From spur to plume a star of tournament,
Shot thro' the lists at Camelot, and charged
Before the eyes of ladies and of kings.
Then loudly cried the bold Sir Bedivere :
" Ah ! my Lord Arthur, whither shall I go ?
Where shall I hide my forehead and my eyes ?
For now I see the true old times are dead,
When every morning brought a noble chance,
And every chance brought out a noble Knight.
Such times have been not since the light that led
The holy Elders with the gift of myrrh,
But now the whole Round Table is dissolved
Which was an image of the mighty world ;
And I, the last, go forth companionless,
And the days darken round me, and the years,
Among new men, strange faces, other minds."
And slowly answered Arthur from the barge :
" The old order changeth, yielding place to new,
And God fulfils Himself in many ways,
Lest one good custom should corrupt the world.
Comfort thyself : What comfort is in me ?
I have lived my life, and that which I have done
May He within Himself make pure ! but thou,
If thou shouldst never see my face again,
Pray for my soul.   More things are wrought by prayer
Than this world dreams of.   Wherefore, let thy voice
Rise like a fountain for me night and day.
For what are men better than sheep or goats
That nourish a blind life within the brain,
If, knowing God, they lift not hands of prayer
Both for themselves and those who call them friend ?
For so the whole round earth is every way
Bound by gold chains about the feet of God.
But now farewell.   I am going a long way
With these thou seëst—if indeed I go
(For all my mind is clouded with a doubt)—
To the island-valley of Avilion ;
Where falls not hail, or rain, or any snow,
Nor ever wind blows loudly ; but it lies

Deep-meadow'd, happy, fair with orchard-lawns
And bowery hollows crown'd with summer sea,
Where I will heal me of my grievous wound."
So said he, and the barge with oar and sail
Moved from the brink, like some full-breasted swan
That, fluting a wild carol ere her death,
Ruffles her pure cold plume, and takes the flood
With swarthy webs.   Long stood Sir Bedivere
Revolving many memories, till the hull
Look'd one black dot against the verge of dawn,
And on the mere the wailing died away.

ALFRED, LORD TENNYSON.

King Arthur's Round Table at Winchester Castle

THE NORMANS

The Normans were great writers and Glastonbury Abbey Library was one of the finest in the world where ancient writing and British History were stored, even Celtic and Welsh History. A joy to see, but now a great loss.

KNIGHT RAYNER THE FLEMMING
AND ROBIN HOOD

The author's ancestor, Lord Rayner the Flemming, under Earl Warenne, founded and endowed a small Priory at Kirklees. Lord Rayner's relative, a Cistercian nun, was installed at the Abbey to keep a close eye on the running of the Priory, and to offer frequent prayers for the well being of the Rayner family.

The Abbess was a cousin of Robin Hood and Robin made frequent visits to Kirklees taking money for the upkeep of the Priory. Kirklees was also a safe haven for Robin when he was away from the protection of the forest and his men.

This cross was worn by the Abbess at Kirklees Abbey

Articulated opening crosses were treasured and cherished over many centuries for holding relics of saints.

THE VATICAN LIBRARIAN

Cardinal Baronius, the great historian and Librarian, in his Ecclesiastical Annals quotes an ancient Vatican manuscript

King Henry VIII, desperately in need of money, ordered the destruction of all Abbeys and Monasteries in England for the only purpose of stealing their wealth accumulated over hundreds of years. The Catholic Church has many scrolls from Glastonbury buried deep in the archives, attesting to the truth in history of Joseph of Arimathea. Last mentioned by the Catholic Church, by Cardinal Baronius, the Vatican Librarian and historian who uncovered the date of AD35. In that year Joseph of Arimathea set sail for England taking with him, Lazarus, Mary Magdalen, Marcella their maid, and Maximum, a Disciple.

THE MANUSCRIPT

The record in the Vatican Library states:. Under the year AD 35, 'in that year Joseph of Arimathea, set sail for England taking with him Lazarus, Mary Magdalen, Marcella their maid and Maximum a disciple'.

'As we know Mary and Martha landed close to Marseilles for safety and to be with Marys family'.

French tradition shows that Lazarus and his sisters; many say the City is 'saturated with them', actually floated into Marseilles to be met by their brethren and taken to safety. Marseilles being the traditional tin routes to Cornwall to the lead mines of the Mendips in Somerset, and visited as part of Josephs Trading Route.

'St. Gildas the Wise' R.I.P.

Gildas lived on the Island of Steepholme off the Coast of Somerset. He chose to live the life of a hermit.

He was a very strong and brave person. Sometimes chased from the Island by pirates, and eventually finding sanctuary close to Glastonbury.

Living by the river near Glastonbury, he built a unique church called 'The Chapel of Happy Retreat'.

He stayed there for the rest of his life where he was buried in the old church near the altar.

THE GREAT SAPPHIRE

One of the most important items stolen from Glastonbury Abbey by King Henry VIII's men was a beautiful Sapphire Altar given by Welsh Saint, St. David. The large centre sapphire from that Altar is in the Crown Jewels.

The reason the Vatican conceals the story is obvious for all to see. Extracts from history recorded in ancient documents throughout the world prove beyond any shadow of doubt that the first Christian Church after the Crucifixion was built at Glastonbury in AD 38 by the Great Uncle of Jesus, Joseph of Arimathea, who used his trading ship to transport Disciples to Britain's shores, at a time in history when there was no church in Rome. Four hundred and fifty years later, the very first Catholic Missionaries came to Britain. And yet the Catholic Church still maintains, without opposition apart from myself and my wife Sylvia, that it brought Christianity to Britain and is consequently the senior church. However, on my side is the eternal quotation from the Bible 'There is nothing hidden that will not be shouted from the highest roof tops'.

AUTHORS NOTE

These last chapters are not an attack or criticism of The Pope, the Catholic Church or Catholics, in any way or sense. I would be the last person in the world who would want to damage any person's faith. My books are about history and historic facts in pursuit of the truth that will set us free.

ST. DAVID OF WALES
THE MYSTERY OF THE SAPPHIRE ALTAR

One of the celebrated treasures given to Glastonbury, the great Sapphire Altar, by our dear St. David of Wales.

St. David gave the Altar to Glastonbury, for he knew the relics of St. Patrick of Ireland and other Saints were treasured here.

'There is an ancient Chapel of St. Patrick still standing in the old Abbey Grounds'

What happened to the Sapphire? Plenty has been written, true reports and cryptics by the Monks.

It is written that when the Cardinal of York was dying in Italy he sent to George the Third in England a great Sapphire, stolen by Henry VIII. Should we look closer at the Crown Jewels? Wales is truly in the Crown of the British Monarchy!

THE SPOILS

In an Inventory of the spoils of Monasteries it - doth say.

'Item: delyvered more unto His Majestie the same day (25th May in the 31st year of his reign) of the same stuffe a superaltare, garnished with silver and gilte, calld the Great Sapphire of Glastonbury'.

The Inventory unique within itself, shows by the description proof that the Altar was portable, a travelling Altar as used by the missionaries in time of War.

St. David and the Old Church

S t. David finding the old Church of Glastonbury built by Joseph of Arimathea and his eleven companions, began to build on the Old Church, in honour of these men who knew Jesus and followed Joseph to the Paradise of Avalon.

Many Saints have contributed year by year to this 'Old Church'. St. David being the first Saint to do so.

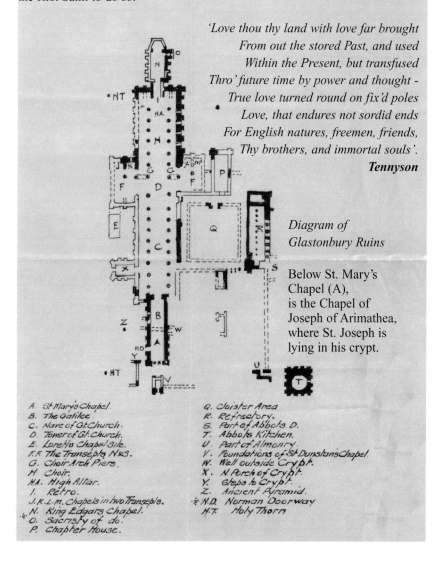

'Love thou thy land with love far brought
From out the stored Past, and used
Within the Present, but transfused
Thro' future time by power and thought -
True love turned round on fix'd poles
Love, that endures not sordid ends
For English natures, freemen, friends,
Thy brothers, and immortal souls'.
Tennyson

Diagram of
Glastonbury Ruins

Below St. Mary's Chapel (A), is the Chapel of Joseph of Arimathea, where St. Joseph is lying in his crypt.

A. St Marys Chapel.
B. The Galilee.
C. Nave of Gt Church.
D. Tower of Gt Church.
E. Loretto Chapel Site.
F.F. The Transepts N & S.
G. Choir Arch Piers.
H. Choir.
H.A. High Altar.
I. Retro.
J.K.L.M. Chapels in two Transepts.
*N. King Edgars Chapel.
*O. Sacristy of do.
P. Chapter House.

Q. Cloister Area
R. Refractory.
S. Part of Abbots D.
T. Abbots Kitchen.
U. Part of Almonry.
V. Foundations of St Dunstans Chapel.
W. Well outside Crypt.
X. N Porch of Crypt.
Y. Steps to Crypt.
Z. Ancient Pyramid.
* N.D. Norman Doorway
H.T. Holy Thorn

THE ABBEY LIVES

Close your eyes and smell the new cut grass,
sweet and perfumed on this hot sunny day.
Back in time, one hundred years ago, the same
grass cutting, the same smell, the joy of
the place and the same uncanny atmosphere.
The Archaeologists, maps, papers, mumbling
and the muffled dig six feet below.

Sylvia Rayner

HOW WAS YOUR DAY?

As I said dear wife it was as spooky as hell.
Tom found the bone rather him than me.

We must have been six foot down when young Tom yelled out
Something like "Land Ahoy" jumped out of skin I did.

The archaeologists became very joyful
Rushing around, measuring, drawing and writing.

And dear wife I have to tell you
It was a human bone.
It was yellow, the arm of a man.

A writer was watching
Nice bloke, Morton I think
Shocked as we were. Historical moment he said.

And dear wife our Tom removed his cap.
And suggested a quick prayer.
We all bowed our heads.

Who was this man?
Saint, Abbot or Arthur. Tom loved that.

It was still light so Tom and Myself celebrated.
Sat on the newly cut grass and had our lunch.

I must say dear wife it was a tasty piece of haddock
in those two crusty chunks.
Still hot from your morning boilup.

We soon had the paper bag of tea, condensed
Milk and hot water in our old bucket.
Out with the army mug.
What a brew!
We both finished with a Gasper.

How was your day?

Sylvia Rayner

*A human bone from the upper arm reported to have been discovered by
archaeologists at Glastonbury in 1927. Attributed to the remains of St. Joseph
of Arimathea. Now in the possession of the Rayner family.*

JERUSALEM

And did those feet in ancient time
Walk upon England's mountains green?
And was the holy Lamb of God
On England's pleasant pastures seen?

And did the Countenance Divine
Shine forth upon clouded hills?
And was Jerusalem builded here
Among these dark Satanic Mills?

Bring me my Bow of burning gold:
Bring me my Arrows of desire:
Bring me my Spear: O clouds unfold!
Bring me my Chariot of fire.

I will not cease from Mental Fight,
Nor shall my Sword sleep in my hand
Till we have built Jerusalem
In England's green and pleasant Land.

William Blake

THINK ON THESE THINGS

Finally, brethren, whatsoever things are true, whatsoever things are honest, whatsoever things are just, whatsoever things are pure, whatsoever things are lovely, whatsoever things are of good report, if there be any virtue, and if there be any praise, think on these things.

ST. PAUL

Finis

HORACE. KNOWLES...

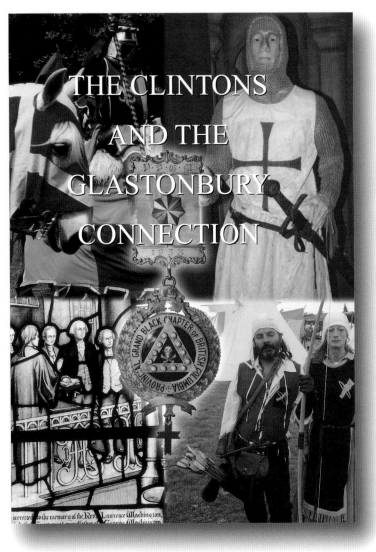

THE CLINTONS AND THE GLASTONBURY CONNECTION

Ronald Rayner
www.theclintonconnection.com   ISBN: 978-0-955-7906-0-7

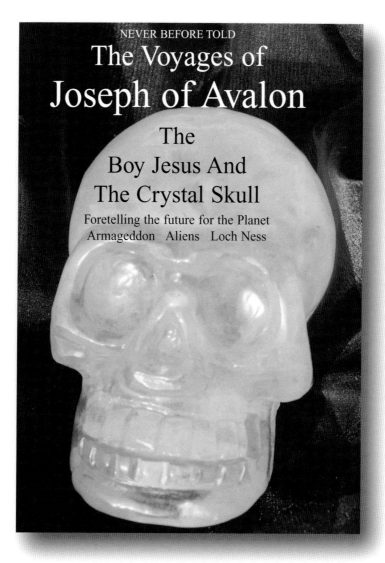

NEVER BEFORE TOLD

The Voyages of
Joseph of Avalon

The
Boy Jesus And
The Crystal Skull

Foretelling the future for the Planet
Armageddon   Aliens   Loch Ness

Ronald Rayner
www.josephofavalon.com   ISBN: 978-0-955-7906-1-4

JERUSALEM 8,500 Years Of History

Walk the path Jesus took down the Mount of Olives almost 2,000 years ago. Take a look at Dominus Flevit, where Jesus wept over Jerusalem. See the Rock of Agony where Jesus prayed while his Disciples slept. Meet Sister Marie as she explains why Jesus was dressed as a King and mocked by the Roman soldiers. Marvel at the beauty of Mary's Tomb and birthplace. Look inside the Holy Sepulchre at the Altar of Nails, the Alter of Crucifixion, Christ's Tomb. Visit the Temple Mount, the Dome of the Rock, the Western Wall and Bar-Mitzvah Ceremonies.

Written, Narrated, Directed and Produced by Ronald Rayner
Assistant Producer Sylvia Rayner.
Programme Running Time 41 minutes approx.
Programme Copyright: © CMB Television Productions. All Rights Reserved.
Package Design & Summary © Blackthorn Publishing Ltd
Visit our website: www.theclintonconnection.com